Silent Cries

Silent Cries

By
Naikiea Jones

FLO'S PRODUCTIONS PUBLISHING SERVICE
An Affiliate of Writers & Self Publishers Association

Genesee County

First Published by Flo's Productions
Website: www.flosproductions.biz
Email: florencedyer@comcast.net
(810) 334-2837

Manuscript and Project by Naikiea Jones
Front & Back Photographs by Wal-Mart Portrait Studios
Front & Back Cover Designed by Flo's Productions

ISBN 0-9769645-5-4

Printed in the United States of America

Dedication

Silent Cries is dedicated to my two cousins: Nailah McLemore (may you rest in peace) and Tenika Moore (waiting for the day we can be close again). Love you both.

To my

BFF fa life love you
hope we never lose touch

Loany

A.K.A

908-4649

From The Publisher

Silent Cries is a true story about abuse, neglect and betrayal. As an Independent Publisher, I have the opportunity to come across a lot of people, who eagerly share their stories with me. Meeting Author Naikiea Jones has been quite an experience. I appreciate her genuine vibrant spirit and the way she views life. Her child like innocence is reflected throughout *Silent Cries*.

There is one question that perplexed Ms. Jones in Chapter VII. I would like answer her by saying, *"I don't know why bad things happen to good people."* All I know is even though situations can be very devastating; God has a way of working them out for our good. What the enemy means for destruction, God can turn it around and make us stronger. I truly admire Ms. Jones. She is an overcomer and has not allowed the abuse she suffered to hold her down.

Reading *Silent Cries,* made me see so much of what we all take for granted. It made me think about holding my children and letting them know how much I love them. There were moments while reading *Silent Cries,* that made me cry. Other times, I had to take deep breaths and set the manuscript aside. Then, there were moments I laughed out loud.

Most of all, I felt privileged to have been given the opportunity to publish the work of a very strong courageous young lady. Through publishing *Silent Cries,* it is my prayer that no other child ever falls prey to another pedophile.

Ms. Jones, I want to thank you for coming forth and sharing your life with the world and me. May God richly bless you in all your future endeavors.

Sincerely,

Florence J. Dyer
Author/Designer/Publisher
Owner of Flo's Productions

Preface

In 1977, an adorable, precious baby girl, full of life was born. As a child, she always thought her life would be filled with love, goals, and happiness. Throughout her adolescence, she always saw life as an educated person who strived hard for the things she wanted. She never thought that unexpected trials would come and turn everything around. She tried to make her life positive but something deep down inside wouldn't allow her to. *Silent Cries* is a true story, Naikiea Jones hopes will open the eyes of every man, woman, boy and girl.

Ms. Jones states, that the abuse she endured led her on a destructive road to hell. She always saw herself as a condom, trying to protect herself from all the bad things in life. For the most part, she viewed herself as a dead girl walking that nobody had buried yet. She often felt very emotional and insecure. She didn't feel wanted from her family, friends, or peers. She looked at other people's lives and wanted to be like them. She feels that fantasy, is what everyone wants instead of reality.

Ms. Jones felt like she was stuck in a system that seemed to suck out her very soul. It seemed as if no one could help her, so she had to help herself. She realized life would go on, even without her. If she wasn't around, who would actually go into a state of depression because she wasn't here anymore? So she had to stop hiding from the truth about different situations and face them head on. She had to figure out what she'd say to people, who had been through what she had lived through. She learned that she couldn't control her life as much as she thought she could. Through her faith in God, she discovered that He controlled her fate, destiny, and how her life would go. God always knew everything that happened to her. He predestined her to go through the different trials and tribulations, so she would be a testimony to someone else. Therefore, it was time to say goodbye to that little girl who had been molested. She had to kick out the teenage girl who abused drugs and alcohol, and used her body as a trash can for the boys.

Finally, she erased the young child who was afraid to open her mouth, and speak up when the chance came to tell who was hurting her. She said see you later, to the young lady who was afraid to commit when someone wanted to commit back. She said, goodbye to the depressed girl who tried to kill herself when things got rough. She had to prepare herself like a woman who had a child to take care of. It was time to set an example for her child. She had to grow, so she would be able to talk to her child about all the wicked things in the world. It was time to step up and finally say no more heartache, no more pain, and no more feeling sorry for herself. She had to learn to trust all over again. Ms. Jones started first with God then she worked her way down. She learned to love, trust, and commit to relationships. Through *Silent Cries* Ms. Jones is here to say, if she can do it anyone can. Betrayal will always be one of the hardest situations to bear. However, with God, all things are possible. Her friends also helped her over come a lot. She also helped them. "*Silent Cries* is her Tears, her Fears, and a Testimony of her life."

Table Of Contents

I
Innocence Shattered

The carefree innocence of childhood is something to be cherished. As I reflect on my own childhood, it grieves me that I was robbed of that precious gift. The molestation and betrayal still haunts me to this day.

I often ask myself; what is the worse thing that anybody could do to me? Now that I am older, that question has been answered. Being betraying by two people, who I never thought would ever betray me, my father and my cousin. I am perplexed by the question of why. Some say for my father, it was the pressure of having to step up and be a man. Taking on the responsibility of a child is a lot of dedication.

As for my cousin, some say he was just plain sick and needed help. The things my cousin did, had me not trusting anyone. According to Webster to trust someone, *is to place confidence or depend on; to confide, and hope to permit, or to stay, or to do something without fear or misgiving.*

My father and my cousin took all that from me and left me wondering, Why? What was it I did so bad to have my father disown me? What did I do to my cousin for him to take my innocence from me? My cousin who was just a child himself violated my innocence. Most people dream of their virginity being broken the night of marriage. I had mine broken at seven. Having to grow up before time was a challenge. Being molested changed my view of the world.

According to Webster Molestation means: *To annoy or disturb. To make annoying sexual advances, to force physical, and use sexual force upon.*

Now I wonder as young as my cousin was what made him do such a thing. I thought, maybe someone had done that to him? If so, why would he return the favor to me? Especially, when it caused him pain and it would do the same to me? I hated my cousin for making me go through so much embarrassment in my life.

Now as I reflect on everything, I don't know what troubled my mind the most; the fact that he was my cousin, or his age. I remember it like it was yesterday. It seemed as if it's a recurring dream and I can't wake up. He would take me downstairs where he once lived, and force himself upon me.

The whole time his mother would be upstairs watching her soap operas (Not knowing that her son was raping me and making me do sexual things that turned him on). He would lay me on the basement floor. The floor was so cold and hard. I would feel him using his fingertips going in between my legs. He would tell me to open wider and relax. He would then hold his penis and guide his way in. I would cry because it hurt so bad. I would also bleed real bad.

It felt as if someone had taken a hard object and just rammed it inside me. He would hold me tight around my shoulders and push himself harder and harder inside me. I would place my hands over my face and hold my breath. I felt such intense pain. I could hardly bear the pain. I knew when he was finished, because I saw this white stuff coming out. That was my clue; he was done doing his business. Afterwards, I would run upstairs to the bathroom and put a pound of tissue inside of my panties. It would hurt when I walked. And, on top of that the tissue would stick to me, from him ejaculating inside of me. Not to mention, I was also bleeding.

The grinding pain, made me feel like everything but a child. It hurt so badly, especially when I had to use the bathroom. My stomach felt like someone had dropped a bowling ball on it. Just knowing that I was lying there having sex, and I couldn't do anything about it, hurt. I hated it, and I hated him. I wondered why me? Here I am a young child without a care or concern in the world. My only dream, at the time, was to become a nurse so I could help people who really needed me. It didn't happen just once, it happened consistently. I felt trapped, not able to do anything. He made me feel dirty.

No one understood the changes that I was going through. I felt they should have. My mother never understood the stubbornness, the change in my attitude or why I had so much hatred in my heart. I always hoped that someone would come downstairs and catch him. At the same time, I thought I would get into trouble too. I felt my family and friends would look at me differently.

I thought they would feel as if, I caused this whole episode that was happening to me. I was scared and just wanted to die. Men became a turn off to me, but in some kind of sick way, I thought this was what men wanted. The way I looked at it as a kid I felt wanted, but dirty. I was confused, not knowing whether I was suppose to like it or not. I thought maybe I did like it. I was going through so many mixed emotions.

I thought this is what I was supposed to be doing. One thing that was clear, what he did to me caused me to grow up fast. The things I would do and say didn't come from me. They came from a child in a crisis that no one noticed or they just ignored. Even though I was a child doing grown-up things, I still had my childhood days. I always tried to put the evil thoughts that I had about my cousin behind me. It was hard considering that I saw him almost everyday. His mother would babysit me while my mom and grandma were at work. I always told my mother, I didn't want to go.

I knew that once my mother left and my cousin's mom's soap operas came on, what was going to happen to me. I guess when you're a child what you want don't matter. When you are that young you don't have a say. Whatever Mom says, that's what happens. Honestly, who would think a child would actually rape another child? In the '80s, it wasn't a big topic that people talked about. I don't believe it crossed anyone's mind that another child could be so deceiving; especially against their little cousin. That was the beginning but not the end of my depression.

II
Broken Pieces

I not only suffered from days of being raped, I also suffered the loss of my cousin that was very near and dear to me.

Nailah was her name. She was three when she died, and I believe when she left this earth a part of me left. Although she wasn't that old, I was still close to her. As a matter of fact, she was the only person I could remember being around growing up with besides my cousin Eric. Her death opened my eyes and let me know that people that you love can be snatched up in a heartbeat. I still wonder why her? She didn't have a chance to grow up and experience life.

Nailah and her family were killed in a car accident on their way home. My cousin Trent was also killed in the accident. I had so many unanswered questions. I was mad at the world and everyone in it. Until this day, I always relive her funeral. I remember seeing a box and my grandma told me Nailah was in it. I kept thinking to myself that she couldn't breathe. I needed to see my little cousin, so I could save her. I wanted to see what she looked like inside the box. I wanted to know what the accident and the people that hit their car did to my cousin. I guess my family thought it was best I didn't see her like that. I needed to see, I needed to feel her pain through looking.

I wanted to kiss her goodbye one last time, and let her know I would never forget her. I wanted to tell her to be my angel and to always keep me in her heart. I never had that chance. As the days, months, and years went on, so did I. I was very confused about death. I never knew why people had to die and leave me in this world, with all the hate that was in it. I thought that she was lucky because she was in a better place, where she wouldn't be hurt anymore. I desperately wanted to be where she was. In spite of the heartache that my mother would have felt, I thought she would have gotten over me.

For the longest time, I was mad at my cousin. I thought; how could she leave me here all alone? I thought these things to myself. Eventually, I gave up caring and just wanted to die. I felt she was in a place where she didn't have to deal with the madness that made me upset. She left me without hope, not knowing where she was or if she was okay. She left me trapped in the world to fight and make it on my own. Her death opened my eyes to accept that people would just leave and I would be alone left with memories.

She left me in a society, where I never believed I belonged. She left me hopeless and to this day, I still wonder why? Grown-ups, in my eyes, don't understand the impact that death leaves on a child. Just like adults children hurt too, maybe even more. I remember spending the night with Nailah. I hated when we had to take a nap. I would probably sleep maybe an hour, when Nailah slept, what seemed like to me forever.

When she was alive, we had so much fun. Nailah was the little sister, I never had. Later it turned into me burying my hopes, dreams; and most of all, my little sister, whom I missed so much. I miss her smile, I miss our friendship and our sisterhood. I longed for years to fill the empty in my heart. I never found it. No one could ever replace Nailah. So I forever hold on to the memories.

III
Bad Choices and Consequences

By the time I was in elementary school, there was a real drastic change in me. It began with, talking back to the teachers, wanting to look sexy but couldn't because I didn't have anything that would make me appear sexy. I wanted to be older than I really was. I being molested. I began having sexual fantasies. I was hanging with a few girls. To be honest, I was too fast for them. They were fighting other girls because they thought they were jealous.

I was also hanging out with the fellas talking about the dumb girls. I remember one particular incident in my sixth grade history class. I should've been listening to the teacher instead I was sitting at my desk making a paper joint. I really don't know what I was thinking when I did that. All I know is the more she talked, the more irritated I became. So I put the joint in the back of my ear, as if I was reminiscing about smoking it. I tilted my head back and closed my eyes. When out of nowhere, the teacher hit my desk, and I jumped. My teacher saw the paper joint behind my ear and asked me, "What is this?" I replied, "What do you think it is?" I really believe she was just getting tired of my attitude.

Well, she sent a note to my mother for her to read and sign. Until this day, I don't remember whether or not I gave the note to my mom or not. All I can remember is the next day; the teacher didn't say anything to me. She was probably fed up with me, had washed her hands and thinking there was no hope. When it was all said and done, I was graduated from elementary.

I was excited that I made it through elementary school and was on my way to Longfellow Middle School. So I thought. Now why did my mother play me? She put me in a private school. I absolutely hated it. I think my mother thought she would really piss me off by putting me in a Catholic Private School. Advise for every parent. If you are not catholic, don't put your children in a Catholic School. I had no business in a Catholic School. I had detention everyday, including Saturdays. I stayed in trouble for playing in Mass Service and talking back. They made us study their religion. I was brought up Baptist. So why should I be forced to learn their religion, worship their God, and take their communion?

One good thing; they were done with Mass in thirty minutes. I guess you could say the school had some good perks. They also took us on a lot of field trips. Other than that, my grades were nothing but Ds and Es. I thought if I got bad grades maybe my mom would take me out and put me in another school. I really underestimated my mom. She told me, I could sit in the 7th grade until I was forty. Which ever came first, I wasn't leaving that school. I wanted to choke her. I even got an E in Religion. I remember my mom asking me, *"How can you flunk religion and you go to church every Sunday?"* I said, *"They are not talking about our God."* I never understood why I flunked either. I knew the Bible wasn't the problem. What I learned about my God and what they taught us about their God was wrong in my eyes and ears. Once I have a mind set on something I believe, I hold on to it, and you can't tell me otherwise.

What was religion to them was different for me. I was taught that when you do something wrong you pray to your Father (God). You ask Him to forgive you, and He will. The Catholics go into a box and tell a man (priest) what they've done, say a few Hail Marys and everything is all right. "Wrong." I remember one time we had to go before the priest. I was ticked, so I made up a story that I killed a cat for no reason. The priest asked me was I sorry? I said no. He told me to do five Hail Marys and all would be well. What kind of crap is that? So as a result of the Catholic School, I flunked religion (Along with other subjects). School was hard for me and I didn't make it any easier. My classmates would laugh at me, when I needed additional help or asked questions. Eventually, I stopped asking questions. I just said, my feelings are worth more than being embarrassed. My learning style required more visual aids. On top of all that, who really uses half the stuff they learn in school anyways? I felt that's why we have the news. I thought, everything you need to know in the world is in the news.

IV
Love, Losses and Disappointments

My mother allowed me to participate in golf and bowling. One of my other cousins was Eric, my hanging buddy. Eric and I were always close but we became even closer in sports. We did everything together, even fought together. We were in private schools together. We felt our parents did us wrong. However, he became my backbone at that time. He was there with me every step of the way. I don't think he ever realized how much I depended on him, at such an early age.

He showed me how to trust again. Out of my trust in him, I loved him. I think Eric and I was around each other so much he knew when I was about to get in trouble, or into a fight. Eric was the only person that could calm me down, and get me under control. I remember once, Eric and I were in his grandma's bedroom. We were wrestling. He called himself giving me a DDT. When he did, he snapped my neck. I thought my neck was broken. So he took a syringe and filled it with alcohol.

Can you believe I was about to let this fool stick a needle into my neck? Well when he was about to inject alcohol into my neck, it squirted into his eyes. He ran around the room crying and covering his eyes. This was just one of the really dumb things we did. When you saw one, you saw the other. I protected him against a lot of things, females, males or whomever. I had his back and he had mine.

I viewed myself as his big sister. I wanted to make sure he didn't feel an ounce of sadness or pain the world had to offer. I had encountered enough for us, and everyone else. So, I stepped up like a big sister and tried to make sure nothing bad ever happened to him. The older we got, the more we had the love, hate thing going on.

Eric and I fought on a daily basis. Eric was the good boy type. He didn't get into trouble. He was sweet and very respectable. He was the guy that every girl's parents would dream about. The difference between us was, I didn't care about anything. I walked around looking for trouble. I ran my mouth so much; I was always into a confrontation. I had a big mouth. Not Eric, he was the type that saved his money, and I would spend mine. He always got on me about spending all my money up. Then, I would ask to borrow some of his. Which, I never paid back. One thing he knew, I would always stay on him about those good for nothing girls, who I wouldn't let take advantage of him.

If the girls he had wasn't up to his standards, I would play interference Often times I broke up bad ridiculous situations. I even hooked him up with my best friend Mandy, who was just like me. Mandy she knew I hated the girl he was going with. I would always tell her to talk to him to break up that relationship. One day, she and I were at the Expo downtown. I saw Eric and his little girlfriend down there. So me being the dirty person that I am, I went over there. I walked up to Eric while dragging Mandy by the arm. I said, "this is my best friend Mandy, she wants to hook up with you."

The whole time waiting for his girlfriend to say something, so I could tear her up. I saw the fire in his eyes. He probably would have killed me, if it weren't so many witnesses. He was angry with me. Like always I get my way, and they did hook up. I guess with Mandy going with my cousin, I could make sure Mandy was behaving, and not playing my cousin. That didn't last long. He finally met a girl. I thought she wasn't right either. Her name was Nerita. I knew her from church.

Nerita, her cousin, and I use to hang together. Somehow we strayed apart. Now, it wasn't that I didn't like her; I just didn't know what her intensions were. Eric really liked her and I realized I couldn't interfere in the relationship. They eventually got married and I really thought it wouldn't work. At the wedding everyone was smiling having a good time. While I was sitting there trying to figure out what her intentions were. I was depressed and really felt she was up to no good.

I guess you can say I didn't want marriage to work. I didn't want her to hurt my cousin either. So I was against it, the whole time. For the first time in my life, I was wrong. It is so strange how we try to protect a person so badly we don't really see when they are truly happy. He married a very sweet person, who I have come to know and love. I respect her a lot. I wouldn't change anything about their life. I wish them all the happiness and love and bad kids in the world. I can finally say, he found the person right for him. Nerita and I have come a long way in our friendship. Our children remind Eric and I of how we use to be. I just hope they both remain as close as we did. Also, I hope they always respect each other and watch out for each other. Most of all, I hope they protect each other from the dangers that may be headed their way.

Eric and I played sports together. Sports became a natural part of me. We were both really into bowling and golf. I loved golf more than bowling. Bowling was a way for me to get out of the house on Saturdays. Especially, since I was always on punishment. One year, Eric and I had the opportunity to bowl in a tournament in New Orleans. Me, Eric, and some other participants were walking down Bourbon Street. I had never seen so many homeless people in my life.

I started to give them money, because they were asking for it. I remember Eric getting mad and calling me stupid. I felt so sorry for them. I just wanted to help them. I guess I didn't understand why these people were living on the streets, dirty and didn't have jobs. My heart ached for them. I wanted to help and give them everything I had. I thought it just wasn't right to walk pass them and not help. Eric, on the other hand, could have cared less about them. I felt I could have helped them. By the time I left New Orleans, I was broke.

Golf was my life. I loved golf. Once again, Eric was right there by my side. We had so much fun together. As I sit and think about it, I don't know who was worse on the trips (Eric and me or our parents). We both have crazy parents. I went on tournaments for both sports. I have trophies, ribbons, and certificates of my accomplishments in both sports. I remember when our golf tournaments were here in Flint, MI. I had to play nine holes on both days. It was hard but I took fourth place in that tournament.

I was proud of myself. My name and picture were in the paper. I always thought that I would join the Women's PGA tour, but as I got older, I found myself being interested in things that I shouldn't have been involved in. I wanted to be with the drug dealers, the high rollers, and the men who had money. I had missed a lot of positive things growing up. I really should have had my head in my books.

I was too busy trying to scheme on my mother, sneaking out the house to hang out and smoke weed. As I reflect back on that time, I hate the choices I made. The main person that I missed, I always wondered did he miss me? My father missed everything there was to know about my childhood. I didn't want any money, all I ever wanted was quality time from him. He had other children, and he didn't spend time with any of us. I look at my life and I blame him, because he should have been there. He was too busy drinking, drugging and hoeing that he didn't even care what I was facing in my life. When I was younger my dad to me, was always will be a loser. He was never there for any of my tournaments.

He was not there to tell the boys that called my house; I was too young for boy phone calls. He wasn't there to teach me to ride a bike or to fight. He was too busy to tell me about the lies the guys would tell, and how to look out for them. He wasn't there for any of my first days of school, or the parent-teacher conferences. He just wasn't there. He wasn't there to kick my cousin ass for violating my innocence. Point blank, he wasn't there.

All I ever wanted in my life was to have a father to talk with. All my friends were doing things with their father. I would just sit with jealousy, because I didn't know where my father was. My mother never saw the tears I shedded because I wanted to be with my father. My mother never dogged my father to me. She let me see for myself just how sorry he was. I love my father so much. I just wanted to cry out and tell him I need him. I needed to know that my father loved me and really wanted me in his life the way that I wanted him. I wanted him to know about all the hurt I was going through.

The pain I felt, about the relationships my friends had with their fathers, was very devastating to me. I wanted him to know the things my family did to me, and most of all, I wanted him to know how the guys mistreated me. I wanted him to feel my hurt and anger. I needed him to hold me in his arms and tell me it was okay. That he would be there to protect me from all the embarrassment, I had gone through all my life. There are some memories I have about my father, but not good ones. I remember when he took me to St. Louis. My mom had bought me a pair of slippers and I wanted to wear them. As we were getting out of the car, I put my slippers on. Well I guess he didn't realize I had them on until we were in the elevator and he beat my butt like it was nobody's business. I was so scared and wanted my mother to rescue me. As I think back, a lot of my memories involve my father whipping me or doing something in front of me (I had no business seeing).

When I was growing up, my dad had a lot of girlfriends. Only two of them I really liked, and they liked me. Brenda, she was the sweetest kindest person you would ever want to meet. She treated me like a princess. Brenda was always buying me things. However, my good for nothing father, would take the credit like he bought it. My mother and I knew better. Now Loretta, she was a person that didn't take no mess off anybody. She always protected me, and saved me when my dad wanted to whip me. She had a son named Lonnie. He and I were like brother and sister.

I loved Lonnie so much, but when my father and his mother broke up we lost touch. I could remember thinking about him when he was gone. My protector

17

had left me. I had to go on with my life and let Lonnie and his mother forever stay a memory in my heart. I remember a poem that I wrote asking questions I felt no one could answer but my father. As I got older, I answered them for myself. These are the questions I asked every night. It took me until I was grown to answer myself:

I guess I always wondered who?
Who would still be around once I poured my heart out?
Who would answer the phone in the a.m. when I needed to talk?
Who would be there to hold me in the middle of the night to tell me it would be okay, when I have a late night dream?
Who would still want to be with you after all the rumors?
Who would still want you when you're considered used up?
Who would still want to be your friend after everyone has betrayed you?
(I guess it was always a question never an answer).
Who would want to commit to a person who was afraid to commit back?
(Once your soul has been taken there is no turning back).
Who would still want to be around you after you have been so depressed that suicide crosses your mind?
Most of all who would be there once you have attempted suicide?
Who would pick up the phone to call you and sit around until you were okay and say, I am here for you?
Who would be there to help you pick up the pieces?
Who will be there to wipe the tears away?
(I guess once again always questions never an answer).

Who would support the decision that I make in my life?
Who would calm me when I'm having an attack?
Who would be there to help me control my moods when I have a bad day?
Who would hold my hand and help me walk through this tribulation?
Who will stand up now and be brave to tell me the truth?
Who is going to sit there and continue to lie?
Who is going to sit in my face and smile than dog me behind my back?
(Still more questions never answers).
Who will be truthful not hurtful?
Who will be caring not deceitful?
Who will be loving not hateful?
Who will be a friend not a foe?
Most of all, who will still love me once my secret is out?

Only one person I know and with Him, I have my friend, love, and trust because only God can judge me now. I have found the answers to my questions. Have you found yours? Who will be in your corner when you have hit rock bottom? *Are you the who, the question or the answer?*

As for my father, I have made a decision on my own. That no matter what anyone says, he is still my father and I will build a relationship with him. He has already missed out on a lot. Is it fair for him to miss out anymore? I don't think so. If there's one thing that my mother taught me, that is to forgive. Without forgiveness than you have no love. Now my heart is ready to love like never before. I guess I look at it just as the Bible says;

That children should obey their parents in the Lord for this is right. And, to honor both your mother and father that this is the first commandment with promise and you may live long on earth.

How can you obey and honor a parent who has never been there? How can I just love and respect a man, who acts as if I didn't exist? There is also another passage that says, *Fathers, do not irritate and provoke your children to anger (do not exasperate them to resentment), but rear them (tenderly) in the training and discipline and the counsel and admonition of the Lord.* (Ephesians 6:1-4)

I look at the passage and feel it was the responsibility of my father to give me the upbringing that would prepare me for life, and would be pleasing to God. It is my parents, and not the church that is primarily responsible for the biblical and spiritual training of me. My father should have raised me with no favoritism with his other children, encourage my good behavior as well as correct my bad. Punish me only in intentional wrong doings, instruct my patience, and dedicate his life to me in love with a heart of compassion, kindness, humility, gentleness, and patience.

Since my father wasn't brought up in church, he was doing things his own way. He couldn't teach me because he didn't know any better. So I still can say, I forgive and love him because that is the Christian thing to do.

V
Guilt, Shame and Regrets

If I were to describe my mother, it would take three different personalities to do that. On one side, when she is real religious and trying to get her point across; she reminds me of Loretta Devine when she played in the movie *Kingdom Come*. She would just yap, yap, yap. When she is in her silly mood, she reminds me of Roseanne Barr with her dry sense of humor. When she is calm, cool and collective she reminds me of Clare Huxtable. But when she is mad, you'd better watch out because all h--- is about to break loose. Remember the movie, *Mommy Dearest* when the lady gets mad about the wire hanger? That is my mom when she is angry (ha, ha). My mother has a very good personality. She is a cool Mother with good values, always respectable and lives a Christian life. I always said my mother has a heart of gold. She will give and has given her last to people. She's a woman who will have your back in any situation. A lot of people tell me my heart is just like my mom's. We would help out anytime we're needed and yet still get burned by people.

My mother was a single parent and she really depended on her family to help us. I was going through many changes. I had reached puberty and having monthly periods. I was still being molested by my cousin. Although my life as a child was not as good as it should have been, considering that I was a child; I thought it couldn't get any worse.

There was a time my mom had to go out of town, and left me at my cousin's house. I did not want to be there. But since, it was just for the weekend, I thought how bad could it be? Upon my mother's return, from out of town, (the next day) I was leaving for a golf tournament in Dayton, Ohio. Once again, my cousin forced himself upon me. But by this time when he finished with me he left me with something. A typical fear for most parents is their children getting beat up by a bully, breaking an arm, or getting hit by a car. What parent would ever have the fear of their child contacting an STD at the age of twelve?

You may have guessed it. My cousin gave me crabs. I did not realize at the time it had happened. I discovered it while on my golfing tournament. I was an irritated mess, trying to concentrate while hitting my ball. I couldn't hit the ball because I was itching so badly. The burning, itching sensation was a horrific experience. I had no idea what the hell was going on with me. I never told my mother about the little tiny bugs that I saw crawling all over my private areas. Now, what else could be going wrong in my life?

I started my period for that month. Here I was twelve, being raped repeatedly by my cousin, dealing with STD, and most of all, being cursed by having a period every month for the next fifty years. Now I didn't think it could get any worse, but it did. Those crabs were killing me, but I was too scared to tell my mother what was going on. I would put Vaseline on all day, everyday.

I shaved my private area, hoping it would go away. I could just feel them crawling all over me. And the longer I didn't tell what was going on, the worse they got. The day my mother found out boy was I relieved. She found out because although I was having a period every month, I was still bleeding from the crabs scratching on my flesh.

Like most parents, she was washing my clothes. She was always finding dirty underwear. She thought I was just being nasty and not taking care of myself during my monthly, but that wasn't the case. I guess she had taken all she could take. She thought I was just being trifling. On this particular night she was in the process of getting ready to whip me. I was crying and trying to explain that I wasn't being nasty, but she really didn't care. At the final second I screamed out, *"I'm not being nasty, I have bugs crawling all over me."*

She stopped, and looked at me. I pulled down my pants and showed her what was left of my irritated and eaten away private area. My granny put some Blue Star ointment on me and in about a week the crabs were gone. Five months of agony, and my mother never questioned what had happened or how did I contract that mess? I never told her. I always wondered, if she had asked me where did they come from, would I have told her?

I had the opportunity to finally stop some of the madness that was going on in my life, but I was too afraid to tell. I didn't know what my family would have thought of me. I was so scared about what she thought of me. I wondered did she think I was having sex?

All I wanted was for her to ask, how did you get that? Then, I could have told here the name of the person who has been violating me for years and it would be all over. I always resented her for not asking me how I contacted crabs. Even now as an adult, I think back on that night, and I wonder, would I have told her what was happening. I had the opportunity to stop that situation, but was too afraid to open my mouth.

Often, people say what they would do or how they would act in a given situation. Believe me when the moment is before you and you have to take a stand, it's not easy. You're nervous and scared of what people will say or think about you. Your nervousness changes a lot. Every time I thought I had enough courage, my heart would ball up. I would think to myself, I blew it again. That would just tear me up inside.

My mother is a strong single parent; however, one thing I hated about her, was she believed whatever people said I did. I got more whippings than a runaway slave. I remember my grandmother pleading with my mom, to just stop the beatings. I was so stubborn and angry that I wouldn't allow myself to cry. I took it like a champ. The pain that I felt from the whippings made me harder and turned my heart hard, where I had anger towards everyone.

I promised myself that I would never whip my children for something that someone else told me. Whether I thought they were capable of doing it or not. There were times she would whip me so hard that I had bruises and had little open scratches, on which she would apply cream on them. I used to be embarrassed when I had to wear dresses or shorts. The children would see them and make fun of me, which made me even angrier. It wasn't just the whipping, if I talked back, she would backhand me in the mouth. One time she missed and it resulted in her hitting me in the nose, causing it to bleed. I didn't have any tissue and she said, I better not thought to myself she crazy. How do I keep the blood from running, and I don't have tissue? My last whipping was in the 8th grade. I was relieved when I didn't have to get a whipping anymore. I looked at the whippings as her toughing me up. I was already hurting on the inside, so the pain from the beatings made me angrier.

I built a wall around me. I would think what I would do to those people that kept hurting me, and not asking what was wrong. Some of the people at my church didn't know that I would daydream about hurting them or even killing some of them. I felt the rage that was building and it was getting worse and worse.

Don't get the wrong impression about my mother. She did the best that she knew how to do with me. I remember when I was younger, I would not fight back. My mother was always getting into it with somebody's child because they would fight me, and I wouldn't fight back. All I had to do was mind her and stop being bad. I had everything I could have dreamed of. She worked two, sometimes three, jobs to make sure I had whatever I wanted.

She is the bomb, and took real good care of me. My mother in my eyes is a person who can take a lot off a person. With her first marriage, I always wished she had a little more patience with him. His name was Norman. I remember when they started dating. He treated me like I was his own child. He was there when I graduated from kindergarten smiling from ear to ear. I love him so much that he was my father. At the time they were together, I never realized it. He never treated me different from his other children. He was there for all my golf and bowling tournaments. He was there at my side every step of the way and I loved him for that.

During storms, he would hold me and calm me from the thunder that scared me. I saw my life as happy, when he was around. I will never forget the day he and my mother were getting a divorce. I cried and cried because the only man I knew as daddy was leaving, and I knew I would never see him again. It took my soul away.

If I ever had the chance to see him again, I know I would just cry out and give him a hug out of this world because I miss him so much. Like the old saying, *"any fool can make a baby, but it takes a real man to be a Father,"* and he was my father always and forever. I was perfect in his eyes. He was my Savior, although I never told him about what was going on, I knew he was there for me. But I was just to frighten to say anything. I didn't want him to think any less of me. He was there for me more than my own father was. It is strange how a man can take a child that is not his and treat them like their very own.

I call that a genuine heart of unconditional love. My own father treated me like someone, he had never met before. Not Norman, he gave me all the love that any child could ever want or need.

VI
Life In The Streets

After the adventures, trials, and tribulations that came in my life, I really just wanted to die. What was left for me to do? I mean, I had been violated, didn't have a father, and had an STD, not to mention losing my cousin. As the months went on, I was around children becoming teenagers.

Their hormones were raging out of control. The guys wanted one thing. All I wanted was all the years I had lost to be given back to me. I had a very belligerent attitude. I didn't care about anything; school, life, or myself. I was a walking time bomb just waiting to explode. The boys that I met were worthless, and I really just wished they would fall off the face of the earth. At an early age, I did meet one, okay, two special guys in my life.

Andre was the first guy I met from church. Most people just saw him as a typical guy that goofed around. I saw ambitions, goals, a sense of humor, honesty, and a natural attraction. I was very attractive to him. He was also attractive to me. It was more of a love-at-first-sight, kind of experience. I literally wanted to take him and show him what I thought love was.

As I grew older, so did my attraction for him. I never thought the day would come that he would be out of my life. I took advantage of the situation because I thought he would always be there. Once you lose a loved one it is very hard to gain their trust again. It wasn't that I cheated on him; it was more that I just couldn't open up and express myself to him. Andre is the only guy that I have ever really loved. Through the experience with him, I know I can form a loving, trusting relationship with someone else.

I was very young when we were together. I really didn't know what a real relationship was at the time. All I knew was that I wanted to be with him forever no matter what, he was my number one priority. Now that I am older, I know what I could have offered him. That is a friend who will always support him in anything that he did in life. Encourage him, when he was feeling like nothing was going right. Most of all communicate and talk about our problems instead of holding them in.

We were not only lovers, we were friends first. Now that I am older, I can open up and express myself and let any man know what he means to me. I always knew how a man should be treated, but my past wouldn't allow me. Most of all, I now know how to listen. I know when to bring up problems and when not to. More than anything, I know how to love; it has been there since day one. My cousin almost ruined my life, but I am glad I was stronger. I did not let it really mess me up. Whether I have Andre in my life or not, I know when my day comes to have a man it will be paradise all the way. Until I find my man, I live off the memories and mistakes I have shared with Andre. I reflect on the right and wrong things, and I correct them and continue to press forward. Out of everything I went through, I did learn that it is not fun being alone. Andre has always been there for me and who could have asked for a better friend than that. I saw Andre as an escape. When I was with him, I never thought about the negative things in my life.

I had been around him for as long as I can remember. Every time he would ask me questions about my father, I would tell him he died in the war. I was ashamed of my father, so I would make him to be some kind of hero. I knew all the time my father was alive. When we got older, the truth came out. Andre never looked at me differently or judged me. I guess you could say, Andre was there to give me a piece of his life. Meaning, I became close to his family. His sister for some reason had to make sure I was always on top of my game.

I couldn't let her find any kind of badness in me. That didn't last long. I saw her as perfect. Her life was running smooth and she didn't have space for garbage. When you are younger, you see things you want to see instead of what is really there. It is like the caution on the mirror of a car which says, Objects are closer than they appear. People's lives aren't as good as they appear. I really thought she would turn out different. Most of all, I thought she would follow the way of the Bible to make sure she reached her goal in life. People's lives are different than they appear. While I was in fifth grade, I met (Kyle) my boyfriend who turned out to be my best friend.

At first I hated him, who eventually became my best friend. Kyle and I became close friends. I trusted him and told him a lot of secrets throughout my life. He was better than any female friends I had. He actually listened to my problems and has always been there for me.

He was a true friend who loved me no matter what I told him, how I acted or what I said. Friends are a dime a dozen, but for me he was there unconditionally no matter what. As I got to know him, I discovered he's a person I can confide in. Even though he and I were close, I didn't tell him what was going on in my life, till years later. Then, I blamed it on my father. I saw it as my father hadn't been there anyway, so why not blame him? Why is it people who have been abused always take up for their attacker? I don't know why I did. Some small part of me wanted to protect him, but a huge part of me wanted to just kill him.

Kyle became my best friend that I was real close to him and loved him dearly. He was always there for me no matter what. He was so young and young minded but he always gave me good advice, and for that I called him my best friend. I never knew how important having a guy as a best friend, would help me in a lot of situations. He would put me up on game that the guys would try to pull. He basically gave me all the inside scope of a man's mind. Whenever I needed him, he was there day or night. I never thought the day would come that I wouldn't have him in my life. When he got into a relationship, I don't believe he knew how to have a girlfriend and a female best friend.

So he cut me off all together. I was hurt. It seemed like everyone I trusted always left my life, and I just couldn't take it or understand that. I was feeling empty and alone and once again, I didn't have anybody to turn to. I always wondered was he thinking about me? My grandmother would always ask me. "Have you talked to Kyle?' I would look at her to say forget Kyle. He had disappointed me in a lot of ways. I really thought of all people, he would always be there. I felt he should have been around during my pregnancy to help me get through it. I guess it hurt more because he didn't see my daughter for a long time.

He was the only one I could rant to and he would take it like a solider. I do believe, I am probably the only girl that could cuss him out and maybe even take a swing at him, and not have to worry about him trying to beat me down. That is a good friend. As much as we argued, hung-up on each other, or cussed each other out, I always thought I would have him in my corner. I had to learn that you can't always control your situations. I just thought he would always control our friendship.

Meaning, no female, he was dealing with, should come between us. I was wrong. I had to put aside my feelings to try to understand what he was going through. I just couldn't, it hurt me to bad every time I thought about him. Once again, I was left feeling empty. Throughout the years, I learned how to deal with things my own way. Whether I got into fights, cussed people out, or gave them the look of death; I learned how to cope with things on my level, which was childish.

I learned that sometimes you can scare a person into silence, than you ever can in words. That just wasn't me. I had to let you know how I felt. I couldn't hold anything in and on top of that, I just had a big mouth. I walked around like I was the untouchable one, I discovered that I had feelings. I thought that I was untouchable and bad, but there was somebody out there who wasn't afraid of me. One day that somebody was going to kick my butt.

Although my attitude was uncontrollable, there was nothing that anyone could tell me. Who were they? They didn't know what I was going through, so I felt that whatever I did was excusable. Besides, I was my own person who wanted to make my own decision, and I didn't care who I hurt in the process. They didn't care if they hurt me. So why should I care about them? If they didn't agree with what I was doing, then screw them. At that point, all I cared about was me.

As I grew older, I saw my attraction to males becoming stronger. There was one problem; I was still this skinny little teenager without a body. Some guys found it attractive. I saw it as an insult. I remember I used to stuff my bra to make my breast look bigger.

Sometimes, I would be moving too much and my left breast would be on my side. Around the age of 13, I saw things getting much harder. I was officially being introduced to drugs, sex, death, and peer pressure. As a teen, either you are mature or immature. Either way you need to know how to handle yourself. Well, I didn't know how to handle myself, so I followed the in crowd. As the months and years went by, I really had the chance to see how guys looked at girls. Very disrespectful, but a lot of the girls: actually thought it was cute. I found myself being with the males more than with the females. In their eyes, I was like one of the fellas. The females I associated with were girls who were flaunting what they had to get what they wanted. I didn't have anything to flaunt, so I used my charms to get whatever I wanted; (Whether it was clothes, money, or respect sometimes even sex if it came down to it).

As I was getting older, I found myself getting into more trouble. The trouble I was getting into caused me to have low self-esteem. I was introduced to drugs at the young age of thirteen. Getting high was like my main priority; (before school, during school, at lunch, or whenever). It seemed like I couldn't function unless I had the feeling that I was getting from the weed. I know from first hand that weed was powerful. Marijuana will have you feeling like you are on top of the world. That is just how I felt. I thought I was untouchable.

Some people look at weed as nothing. We feel that it doesn't have an effect or that it's a power cigarette. It is more than that and I was on drugs real bad. Hanging with the crowd, I learned a about drugs (weighing it, bagging it, even cooking it). It became a natural and a very bad activity. I was happy doing what I was doing. That's what I wanted to do. It made me feel like I was in control of my life. It gave me a rush, and most of all, it just made me feel good. I was always at somebody's drug house. A lot of people knew me from doing dirt. I wasn't a dumb female; I caught on real quick to the dope game. I hated to apply my good knowledge when it came down to positive things. I couldn't walk around like some nerdy girl.

I had to always be on top of the game, when it came down to the streets. I figured out what to do and how to make me some quick money. What did I need with an education? The everyday hustle that I had was going to either have me dead or in jail. I figured if I get caught, at least I wouldn't keep getting hurt by people. In the back of my mind, I felt I was too slick for that and really thought I could talk my way out of anything. On and off, I sold weed from time to time. I use to do nails in my mothers basement, to hide some of the money that I had in my pocket. My mother never knew the bags of weed I had in her house or in my car.

I would ride around with weed in my car. Then, I would come home and bag it up. Sometimes I would have to make sure I came in late, so my mother would not catch me bringing it into the house. I was really stupid and most of all, uneducated. However, it put money into my pocket, and gave me trust from many guys who I would get my supplies from. They trusted what I did and what I knew. They knew that I would never snitch on them. We had a pack whatever I heard or saw it would be taken to the grave, and I have kept that promise since day one.

I learned a lot from the streets. A most important lesson was that I am a very intelligent person, and was dealing with people who could contribute very little to my well being. I was smarter, than the guys who thought they could control me. I now know that I allowed them to, but I was really in control.

The street smarts that I had were bringing my life to an end. I was always in some confrontation, whether it was with males or females. What I saw was hatred. I had everything I needed for a teenager, and then some. Going with different drug dealers that constantly kept money in my pockets, clothes on my back, and all the jewelry I wanted. I had to camouflage my clothing, so my mother would not ask me where I got certain outfits. I would put clothes in my book bag and change on my way to school. Which didn't leave much time to change considering my school was right around the corner. What people thought about me, I didn't care.

I had been around and seen too much; drug busts, jumping out of windows, get-a-ways, drive bys, people trying to kill my boyfriends. I was terrified. I would ask myself, what are you doing? What I thought was protection from these so-called boyfriends I had, wasn't. They could have killed me just to get to them. Who's to say, that I would have even cared if I was dead. I wasn't aware at the time that I could have been a target from what I had seen or been around.

I know what I thought was love from these guys was nothing but disrespect. I didn't have enough sense to see that and get away from them. The guys were very disrespectful and the girls thought it was cute. I would just wish a guy would talk to me the way they talked to some girls, so I could blow their jaw out. If there was one thing my mother taught me, it was not to let anybody talk to you any kind of way. I made sure guys respected me whenever they spoke to me verbally. I was an only child, so I had to learn to protect myself. I didn't play that.

One guy I went with, for about two or three years was a drug dealer. My mother may have suspected it but she never confronted it. I told her he was sick a lot and on disability. Which was the truth. My aunt, by marriage, was his cousin. So she told my mother that he was a drug dealer, and that when he smoked weed, it would mess with his sickle cell disease. I wanted to tell her that he didn't smoke weed. I was the one smoking weed, so shut up if you don't know what you are talking about. He had a disease called sickle cell anemia. So he was always in the hospital.

When I first met him, he was real cool. It wasn't anything that I couldn't ask him for. While I was with him, I was a candy striper at the hospital. Before I knew it, I didn't have time to go to the hospital. So while my mother thought I was at the hospital, I was really with him. Most of the time, my girls and I would be smoking up his weed, and I would steal some for me later. My friends and I, would go over his house with the music blasting, smoking and making my ex boyfriend who stayed across the street from him jealous I remember once, when I was in the eleventh grade and I was skipping a class, he came up to the school and brought me flowers and a stuffed bear for Valentine's Day. I thought I was something, having this grown man bring me gifts up to the school. Being with him, I saw things and learned things. I learned even though I thought I loved him, I couldn't have. You don't pull a gun on someone you love.

Since he was in and out of the hospital, I had other guys I was with. Especially, the cousin of the girl that I hung with all day, everyday. I was going with her cousin. It wasn't anything sexual with the guys I was with; we would just sit back and smoke his weed. By him always being in the hospital, I was always there with him and I really felt I was too young to give him the kind of attention he really needed. Guys knew I was talking to him. They would sometimes try to run game and tell me the dirt he was doing in the streets with other females. I couldn't get mad because I was doing the same thing.

I would be at the hospital all day. That was really cutting into my hangout time with other males. Not to mention, I was supposed to be at the hospital doing my candy striper job. Sometimes I would tell him my mother wouldn't let me use her car. People would see me out riding with guys in the car and go back and tell him. I didn't care, the way I saw it was; may the fattest pocket win. He couldn't give me the attention I needed, so I went elsewhere. One day I was over his house, when I should have been at the hospital. We had a bad argument that almost cost me my life.

I really wasn't trying to hear what he was saying. I felt, I am young and had my own friends. I couldn't really be tied down with one man. Well while he was fussing, I figured it was time for me to go. He wasn't even trying to hear that. So while I was going to the car and leave, he pulled out his gun and said, *"If you leave I will kill you."* Now anybody in their right mind would have been scared. That was the problem; I wasn't in my right mind. I looked at him with this smirk on my face, as if to say I dare you. I really didn't know if he would shoot me or not. I dam sure wasn't going to let him know that I had fear in me. So I took a step back looked him square in his eyes and said, *"If you're going to shoot me, do what you do. But like I said, we will talk later."*

He then snatched me up and said a couple of choice words and, once again, with the same smirk on my face I said, "I will talk to you later." I got into my car and left. All the time this was going on; my ex boyfriend saw the whole confrontation, and still to this day, he likes to throw that in my face. Like I said, I was young and dumb. To me it was a rush. I didn't know whether or not he would pull the trigger and I really didn't care. I was at the end of my rope. Who would care, if I was gone? I was at the point that you couldn't kill me because in my eyes, I was already dead. My soul had been burned, ripped out but not buried. I had died back in 1985. It was just that no one had buried me. I was lost, hurt, and betrayed. So why not pull the trigger? I was already gone.

Maybe this time, they would put me in the box and throw the dirt on me. After I left, I thought I must have a serious problem. Here I am with this grown man, and he is threatening my life and I was actually getting a rush from it. I really didn't have any business trying to play the role as a woman with a man. I thought it was cute. I was so stupid. I never thought what happens if this fool does pull the trigger and shoot me. What happens if I come home and my mother windows are shot out? What can I say to her about what happened? Well from that day, I told myself that I refuse to be on of those girls out in the streets that lets a man put fear in their heart.

I wasn't going to be a victim of domestic violence because some man had a problem with his manhood or ego. I dam sure wasn't going to let a man put fear in me with a gun. One thing that I learned in church was, "God has not given us the spirit of fear but of power, love, and a sound mind." I wasn't brought up in fear and I wasn't going to live in it. My stubbornness wouldn't allow me to swallow my pride and run when trouble came my way. I had it in my mind, either beat them down or get beat down. The hurt that I had in my heart had my brain stuck on evil. Not to mention, I was addicted to two artist that were devil worshipers (Esham and Natas). I loved and worshiped them. I was evil and very mean. I didn't care if I offended or hurt your feelings. It was my way or no way. No questions asked.

VII
Trials and Tribulations

Throughout my life, I found out who my friends were and who my foes were. What is a friend? Now some people think a friend is just a person who may have your back, or lie for you when you are in a tough situation. According to Webster a good friend is *a person who trusts, likes, or even knows. A favored companion, or acquaintance. A person who supports, sympathizes with, or patronizes a group, cause or movement.* According to Webster a foe is *a personal enemy. An adversary or opponent. Something that serves to oppose injures or impedes. In other words not a friend.*

Both of these play a big role when you are trying to form a relationship. As I started to mature, I found out who my friends were and who my foes were. My so-called friends were the ones whom I was getting into trouble with. The ones who I got high with and really thought they had my back. These friends or foes go all the way back to my childhood. Those I thought were my friends were the same girls who were dogging me behind my back. There are three so called friends in particular. One girl, I had known since junior high. She introduced me to drugs in the 7th grade. The other girl I met in school. Now the three of us hung like thieves.

You never saw one without the other two. The day I found out they weren't my friends all hell broke

40

loose. A rumor about me being gay was going around. This one particular senior who liked me got upset because I wouldn't have sex with him. He was fine as h--- too. But I had heard about the entire little sex rumor about him, and was not about to become a victim of his sex stories. Anyway, I turned down his offer so from that day forth he told everyone I was gay.

Considering that was the worse rumor I had heard about me, no one paid it any attention. Even though the rumor was out, I knew I wasn't gay. Well years passed on and my so-called friends and I were starting to stray apart. We still talked, but things weren't like they used to be. One day, I was coming back from the Skill Center. I had spoken to them, but they just looked at me and gave me a dry "hi." So I came back and asked them what's up. One of them caught an attitude and made a comment about me being a dike.

So I said to her, if I am a dike then what does that make you? They were both always at my house. So if I'm a dike so are you. Instantly, I got upset. Before I knew it, I rammed her head into the steel door at school. From there it was on and popping. Honestly, I was trying to kill her. I punched her until, I couldn't punch any more. After that we never spoke again. I always wondered what really escalated between the three of us? They were my girls. At least I thought they were. They were the ones I told my secrets to. The ones I invited to my house, and most of all the friends that I trusted. It took a while but I finally saw that they were not my friends. I believe that was the first time my feeling had ever been hurt over some females. It sure wasn't the last time. To feel the betrayal and heartache from them finally let me see that I did have feelings. As the years went on, I found out that the people that I called friends were foes, and some of my foes were actually my friends. That was an eye opener. When I grew up, I started to get into more serious relationships with my friends and even guys I called boyfriends.

I was always in and out of relationships. It had gotten to the point that, once again, I was rebelling against my mother. As I was growing up there were three girls that I really admired and I don't think they had a clue. We attend the same church. The day I joined the choir is when I really noticed them. I knew I wanted to be like three girls in my church. When I was younger, they were people I looked up to and wanted to be like.

When you're younger you look at people and think their life is just perfect. You never know what they may be going through. I watched their every move and studied them like they were a homework assignment. Nikki, had more of the; I don't care attitude. She kept to herself and minded her own business; she was what I thought of as a very rare gem. When I was younger, I really wanted her to notice me. It was as if she didn't know I was alive, but I never stopped admiring her no matter how she didn't notice me.

She became pregnant at a young age. I heard a lot of people talking about her. I must admit they made me angry, and I would defend her every time. I looked at her situation and she turned it around. She raised her son with the help and support of her parents. She graduated from high school and college. I considered her to be an idol and a hero. I always wondered how she did it? How she kept her mind straight and still managed to be a very successful woman today. I know it was God and her dedication to what she knew she had to do in life. I stand up and I applaud her for all her hard work.

The Tonya is a friendly and a loving person and she on the other hand did notice me. I love her like a sister that I never had. I never had the courage to let her know how much she influenced my life. She is now a minister. In Bible Study Classes she often testifies about her past, which sounded a lot like mine. With God's help she is now a very power woman. She has helped me turn my life around. I owe a lot of my maturing to her. She took time to show me the destructive path I was on. She showed me the right way to go. I love her so much. She told me that I can excel in life and that my past is just that a past tense of what I used to be. Tonya has shown me how to look towards the future. How to depend on God and ask him for guidance. Most of all, she showed me how to be me, and if people can't accept me its okay because they didn't accept Christ either. (She sounded a lot like my mother).

With Felisha, there are really no words to express what I felt for her. She was the sister of the person that I fell in love with. She was also a person that as I got to know her, I became protective over her. Anything that I did, I wanted to make sure it made her happy in some kind way. It was as if I went out of my way, to make sure I didn't do anything to let her down. I love her with all my heart and it wasn't anything or any limit that I would go to make sure that whatever I did made her proud of me. Sometimes I would do things that would let her down and also myself. When I was pregnant I couldn't tell her. I didn't want her to think any less of me. Therefore, I kept that secret for as long as I could.

I looked at it as the way my life was going; she probably had an idea that I would become pregnant. With her, it seemed like the more I would fight and protect her from people hurting her, she would turn around and do something to hurt me. I guess you could say I tried to ignore and when people tell me some of the things she said about me. Deep down it was killing me. Just to know she would say negative things when I wasn't around, really hurt me; especially, when the things were not true.

I would have liked her to come to me as a sister instead of talking behind my back. In spite of it all, I still love her. I have learned not to take up for her anymore, to just let her handle her own problems. I will always be a friend and a sister to her. I feel it's the right thing to do. I try to look at situations on how God would handle them. Then I realized, I am not God, so I handled things childishly. See with the first two girls, it really didn't matter if they knew I was alive or not, but with the third girl I guess you can say I tried even harder for her to notice me. As I got older they began to accept me in spite of the way I acted, the things that I said, or even the things I had been through.

They were my friends and my family and I wouldn't let anybody talk bad about them. In return they did they same for me. See with my other so called friends, I did things to please them. While on the other hand, all I had to do was be myself and with that most people are satisfied. As the years were passing, I saw a change in someone I thought was my sister. Her attitude towards me wasn't the same. She would talk about me behind my back, and then act as if she never said it.

I was beginning to see how fake she was, and I was getting tired of trying to act like I didn't know she was dogging me to other people. I would jump hurdles to make her happy, or prove my loyalty to her, but what's the point? She doesn't respect or love herself. So how can I expect her to love and respect me? Now I just handle her with a long handle spoon.

I thought that you do what you have to do to prove yourself to a so-called friend or boyfriend. I did just that by sneaking out of the house and stealing my uncle's car. It took me years to realize that they didn't respect nor did they love me. The so called friends that I had were like snakes. I was good for them when they needed me for money, to borrow clothes or wanting a ride. At times it hurt, but then I realized they needed me. No longer was I doing anymore freebees for my foes.

Don't sit and look at me strange because we have all been used by someone at one time or another. Well the months went on, and I had started this so called dating process. Every guy that I dated was always older than I. It was a challenge to me. The guys I went out with, we found out that we weren't meant to be. So we just said it was better to be friends. My first love, that I think about a lot, got away. Every time I saw him, it was this nervousness that came over me.

I always felt as though I wasn't good enough for him that I would never meet his standards. It took me a while to get that feeling out of my mind. I knew I was the one for him and still believe that in my heart until this day. We went together off and on, but I really thought when I got older and more settled, I could always have him back into my life. Does it make me upset sometimes yeah it does. I have regrets about what could have been. However, I am older and much more mature, and I learned from the mistakes that I made with my relationship with him. People can always assume things, but what is the point of assuming that you think a person know how you feel about them, when you can just be woman enough, and tell them how you feel. We shared a lot of memories, going out to eat, movies, and just spending time together. Most of all, we shared a wonderful friendship that will never leave. When I finally got the guts to let him know how I really felt it was too late. It was my own pride and scariness that left me alone and some other woman has my man.

Am I angry? Yeah! However, you grow up and you move on. Then you put on your fake smile and wish them nothing but the best. One thing I know for sure the next man I fall in love with, I won't let him get away. If I haven't learned anything else I have learned that it is not fun being alone or loving somebody who doesn't love you. I knew my family loved me, but I guess they are supposed to, they're family. Although my cousin is perverted other members are real cool. I only have a select few in my family that I deal with.

Family is supposed to be close, loving, forgiving, and most of all family. But our family didn't have that. You had one group that didn't talk to the other group. I mean, it was hard having family gatherings when some people were not talking to each other or didn't show up. The biggest confusion came when my cousin and I were around. We never really saw eye to eye and it was probably because we didn't grow up together. She was closer to our cousins from the south. It was nothing in this world that would have made me happier, then to have a good solid relationship with my cousin.

It is important to know that you always have family that got your back or someone who you could depend on, and you could give them the same in return. The reason that she and I weren't close wasn't all her fault. There are some things that I could have done differently. I would go tit-for-tat with her whenever she did mean things to me. Which didn't make either of us right or wrong. I used to live with her when she stayed in an apartment around the corner from where I live now. I moved in with her to help her out with her daughter.

She worked a lot and I took it upon myself to help my family out. I would get up in the morning feed her daughter, get her ready for school, and be there to pick her back up. My cousin worked second shift and sometimes when her car was not running, I would let her use my car. Which meant, I was stuck in her house without a car until she came home. I would lie to my mother about where the car was. When she came by I would say, it's parked somewhere else. I really didn't mind her using the car.

Just to know that I was helping out and being not only a good friend, but doing what family should do for one another. Even though my cousin didn't find out what happened to me until years later, there was still a separation between us. She always took up for him, which made me believe that he violated her too. I never asked her, but I have a feeling he did. She probably wouldn't tell me if it did happen. It was like a division. We hung with the same people and could not get along. As long as we were alone, we got along find. I always felt her friends influenced her.

Some of the girls she was hanging with were bringing her down. I learned how to separate myself from them. I saw the change and affect her friends had on her and just said, skip her. Who needs her anyways? I wanted to show her, there were other people that she could be with. I just said forget her. I always wished we could have been like best friends. I love her always that will never change. Maybe one day we will be able to be good friends.

We can start to trust each other and build a good solid relationship. I hope someday soon! Now I look at it as I have a new family; my church friends and their families are my new adopted family. I would truly bend over backwards to make sure they are happy. I love my family and wish that we could all get along with each other. I know you can't pick your family, but I feel you have to make the best out of anything regardless of your feelings. As the years went on and I left people that meant me no good, I tried to put my life together.

I remember one relationship that I had with this guy. In the beginning, I did love him or at least I thought I did. He really wasn't my type, but in the beginning we had a lot of fun together. We use to go to Detroit a lot and just hang out. He was very sweet. After about a year, we started to argue a lot. My biggest issue was he never had any money.

I paid for a lot of things whenever we went out. On top of that, he never had anything decent to wear which embarrassed me, to be out in public with him. We had gotten into a bad argument. I said I didn't want to be with him anymore. So another guy I had been involved with for about a couple of weeks, we started to hook up and spend more time together.

I was already talking to this man, while dating him. I can't even lie. It was fourth of July weekend and everybody was hanging out. My friend and I were at my house chilling. My cousin who was trying to get me and my boyfriend back together called me from the club. I blurted out that I had just had sex with this guy. She acted as if she didn't hear me, so I repeated myself. Next thing I know she hangs up the phone on me. She called back about ten minutes later to tell me my old boyfriend was on the phone with her. I really didn't care. I was tired of him. The next day my cousin talked me into seeing to him.

That stupid fool pulled a gun on me. How do I meet these stupid guys? We got to arguing and I just left. I didn't have time for his foolishness. Once again, I thought it was cute, and I had to tell everyone he pulled a gun on me. I was so special. For some dumb reason, we managed to get back together. Not only that, we managed to go off to school and live together. Our first night together we go into it. A group of us were on our way to an icebreaker at Northwood University. We all piled into my car. We were drinking, and my friend and I were smoking some good weed. My boyfriend started to get irritated about me smoking weed. I know he hated when I smoked but that's me. Deal with it.

By the time we had got to Northwood, we were arguing about who knows what. We got out of the car and he called me a B----, and said, "If I knew you were going to be acting like this, I would have left you're a-- at home." I could have caused a scene, but I got in my car, left him and everybody else that was in my car. I drove back to Mt. Pleasant by myself. I knew he didn't have a key to the apartment yet. He called all night asking if I was going to let him in. The answer was no. I can honestly say, I had one good night of sleep.

Days and weeks went on and I saw things were not working. Once again, instead of just separating myself from him, I just did more things to piss him off. I started hanging out later, using more drugs, and drinking more. I had met a girl from school and she had become my hanging partner. She was real cool not only that, to pay for her schooling she became a stripper. I heard all the stories that she would tell about stripping, and I must admit it turned me on.

So I found out how I could do just that. She was stripping down in this club in the D. I found myself down there with her almost every weekend. So later I tried it out for a while. I really wanted to see what it was like. I must admit that was the most degrading experience I had ever encountered. The things that we did for a dollar or for ten dollars, and even worse, what could happen in the VIP room.

I must be honest, that was nothing that I could have done sober. So I made sure I was higher than high. I would be so drunk that I could hardly hold my balance to get up on the stage to perform. That lasted about a month and a half and I said that's not for me. My boyfriend had figured out that I might be stripping but really had no proof. So one night, I was going to this bar at school called the Way Side. It was a little mixed bar that we all went to. As I was leaving to go to the club my so called boyfriend told me to be home at 2:00 a.m. Being who I am, no one puts a time limit on when I make it home.

Especially, if you're a lazy behind, can't get a job and support us. So I got there when I got there. He must have been pretty bored and angry at the same time. He had the nerve to unscrew every light bulb in the apartment. When I had arrived home, I came in to turn on the light and there was no light. There he was standing in the corner of a dark apartment talking about he had unscrewed all the light bulbs. So I just came in and was about to go to bed.

He was really angry and wanted to argue. We got to fighting and I was throwing stuff. When I say fighting, I mean we were fighting like two people who had never seen each other before. After a while, I figured enough was enough, so I got into my car and prepared to leave. He followed me outside and jumped in front of my car. My mind was telling me don't do it. But I thought I was justified for him hitting me.

So I pushed the petal to the metal and ran his sorry worthless behind over. Not thinking I just kept going I was so high and so drunk. I wasn't thinking and just did my first instinct. I came back home to get me some clothes to stay the night with a friend. When I got back the police were there. Now you know we were in a white town. The police were there in five minutes. Would you believe I got arrested? You talking about somebody mad and upset. Now, I don't know who ever said jail was a place to be, but I knew that was not the place for me.

It was the longest, hardest, thing that I believe I had ever encountered. There was this gay girl in the cell with me. She was coming on to me and everything. So I figured if you think you are going to hold me down and try to get some then it was going to be the nastiest sex you ever had. She kept starring at me and trying to grab all over me so I did the best thing I knew to do. I used the bathroom all over myself. Then I sat there with a smirk on my face. And looked at her and said now what you go do?

I wasn't going to make her raping me that easy. I was finally released, had anger management classes, and was almost banned from Mt. Pleasant. Believe you me, that wasn't the first time we fought and it definitely wasn't the last. I saw that this was going to be a problem; there wasn't a day that went by that he and I didn't throw some blows. So I said, enough was enough, I packed my stuff and left. When I finally arrived home the Mt. Pleasant Police was looking for me. When I was at school there was a girl taking credit card numbers from people. One day she called me on the phone, and asked me to come to her job, which was Meijer, and do some shopping for her. She said that she was working late, and would be tired when she got off. Plus, she said that they were running low on groceries and asked me to pick up a few things and take them to her sister. I wasn't doing anything, so I did it for her. I was stupid, because now I wonder why her sister didn't just go get the things herself.

Now it's too late for the should've, would've could've right now. Anyway, I went there and got the list of things that she claimed she needed. I got the items came back to her line and she gave me her credit card. I know for a fact it was her card, because it had her name on it. She claimed that the slider on her card didn't work, so she punched in the numbers. What did I know? I didn't know it was the numbers she punched in were from someone else's credit card. She had taken those numbers when another customer had used a credit card. Well when the police caught up to me, they told me about the fraudulent crime that I had committed.

I really had no idea what they were talking about. So when I went back to Mt. Pleasant they explained what was going on. Well to make this long story even shorter, I had to go to court. I received probation, community service, and had to pay back a large sum of money neither me nor my mother had. During the time I was on probation, I found out something that was very disturbing. I discovered I was pregnant, and it ticked me off. When I found out I was pregnant the first thing that came to mind was I wanted an abortion.

The second thing was my mother is going to be so mad at me. Most of all, I thought about what would Felisha think of me. Here I was trying to be this perfect person in the eyes of someone I looked up to, and I had gotten pregnant by somebody I really didn't want back in my life. So for six months I hid my pregnancy from everyone. In my fourth month when I felt abortion was the best thing to do I felt my baby move. I must admit it touched me that I had a person inside me that was living, breathing, and most of all moving.

I made the decision to tell somebody, so I called a close friend. I knew if anybody could relate to what I was going through it would be her since she had been through a similar situation as mine. When I called, I was basically down to nothing but tears. I told her I didn't know what to do. She supported me in whatever it was I wanted to do. There was just one problem, I still did not want the one person that I looked up to, to find out that I had made another mistake and gotten pregnant. I made the decision to get an abortion.

I made my appointment to go to Detroit for the abortion. Can you believe when I got there the doctor had called in sick. I was so disappointed. I figured God must really want me to have this baby because everything I thought to do just back fired. I hid my pregnancy for the longest. I only shared my pregnancy with one of my closest friends. She never discussed me being pregnant to anybody. I believe she thought I got and abortion. One Sunday I was at church.

My little sister Angel walked up to me and said you are getting fat. She then started poking me in the stomach and said, "Why is your stomach so hard? Are you pregnant?" I said, "Yes Angel don't tell anybody." She said, "Okay" Before I could get home my pager was blowing up. That day when the phone rung and it was Felisha on the other side my heart dropped down to my feet. My mother, I knew she would forgive me and support me and my child.

However, I didn't know what the person I admired would think of me. Well to make our conservation go a little smooth I burst out and said, "I want her to be my baby's godmother." What else was there to say? Well, the months went on and during my pregnancy I found out I had abnormal cells in my cervix. I was getting biopsy, after biopsy, which was very painful. Finally, I had gotten to the point the doctors explained to me what was going on. He said, my cells look like cancer cells. After I heard that I went straight into panic mode.

I had set in my mind that I wasn't going to tell anybody because I didn't want anyone to worry and I didn't want people to start acting funny over me. So I kept it a secret, which was very hard for me to do. Especially, when I can't hold water. My pregnancy I would say was a blessing. I know that it was meant for me to have my baby. I went through hell and hot water not to have this baby. I had to adjust myself and get mentally prepared to becoming a mother. In a way, I was glad. I was eating everything that wasn't nailed to the floor.

I went into labor three times, and my grand mother was the one who always drove me to the hospital. On a normal day, I would care if my grand mother was driving me. There was one problem by expressway, the hospital was about 20 minutes away but my granny didn't drive on the expressway. She took the long way from Flint to Holly. I was so mad at her. When it was actually time for me have the baby I was nervous. I will never forget going into labor. The worst experience I had ever gone through.

I actually had her without an epidural. Now I wished I had one. I was in labor for about five hours. I remember when it was getting close to deliver; I didn't want to hear anyone talk, breathe, or sigh. I was in the middle of a contraction and my mother was on the phone running her mouth. I wanted to snatch that phone right out the wall. I remember a close friend looking at my mother and telling her, I think you better get off the phone. I was in too much pain to do anything.

It had come a time, I wanted some water and the nurse brought me some ice chips. I gave her the look of death. I asked her what do you think ice is, frozen water stupid. She was really asking for it. Between my mother and my little sister Angel, I wanted to kill them. My mother was running her mouth, and Angel was snapping pictures every five minutes. Well, we're down to the last 10 minutes.

The pain was getting worst every minute. I swear I felt bones breaking. When she was crowning, I thought I had to use the bathroom. I was fighting the nurses trying to rush to the bathroom. They told me it's time to push. I pushed four times and there she was. Taylor AiYanna Jones weighed 6lbs.1oz. My first thought, was this girl is ugly she looked like a wet rat.

Through all the pain, every cry, every scream, and every contraction, my friend was right there helping me through it. When I thought I couldn't do anymore she told me I could. I was at the point to where I was literally pulling my hair out, and she held my hand, and helped me all the way. She showed up in a way, I never would have imagined. It was a good thing she was there because my mother wouldn't have been able to handle it. After about a week, I had the most beautiful chocolate baby in the world.

After all the trials with my pregnancy, my friends and family really helped me like they said they would. I believe I had the baby for them. I remember Taylor was crying and crying. I didn't know what was wrong with her. I couldn't find my mother or granny. My other friend wasn't answering her phone. I was upset crying on the computer about to put her up for adoption. I called Jamise at work. I remember crying and yelling to Jamise that she wouldn't stop crying; that nothing was wrong with her. I had fed her, changed her and everything.

The whole time both of us were crying; Jamise told me to put the baby down and calm down. After she got me under control she asked me have you burped the baby? I did and she stopped crying. I remember Jamise telling me when I was upset not to shake the baby. I thanked God my friend was at work and in her office at the time. I have the best support group a girl could ever have.

I honestly don't know how young girls do it. Babies require a stable person to raise them. I mean I was 23 when I had her. It seems like girls are getting younger and younger having babies and it is so hard trying to read the mind of a little tiny person. I applaud any young person that has a baby. If it was hard for me at 23 I know what they are experiencing. After Taylor was about four months old my doctor decided it was time to do something about my abnormal cells. Everyone thought I was just going in to get my tubes tied which I did, but I also had half my cervix removed which was the affected area. After which I was cancer free.

I was so happy, I thought to myself God had spared my life once again. No matter what kind of disease you have or whether it can be fixed or not, just to hear that you may have cancer is scary enough. I was so stressed out, and nervous. My biggest fear was me loosing my hair. I believe I prayed more during that time then in my whole life. I don't know if I could have gone through that experience. I was so glad I didn't have to. Now that my baby is here she is the best thing that happened to me. She slowed me down a lot. She made me realize the irresponsible things I was doing. I had to stop because I wanted to see my child grow up. I am very protective of my baby.

Mainly because I don't want her to go through what I went through during my childhood. If I could give advice to anyone it would be, not to have sex before it is time it can wait. A child is very expensive and requires a lot of patience and most of all two parents. If I had the chance to do it all over again, I would be married and financially stable to take care of my baby the way I would like to. I always promised myself I would never spank my child the way my mother did me. That didn't work. Taylor will get that butt spanked when she needs it, which isn't that often. I read so many books on how to raise a child.

Out of all the books in the world, there is only one book that can help you raise a child, and that's the Bible. I love my child more than myself. I have committed myself to be a responsible parent to my child. To love her and give her everything that her heart and mind could ever dream of. So far I have managed to do just that and without the help of State Assistance. I had to stop doing things like smoking around her because I didn't want her to grow up fast like I did. Taylor has been to almost every state in the U.S.

I want my child to have the experience of other things in the world. I don't want her to think that

Flint, MI is where her life ends. I want her to grasp the world and explore it. I treat my child like she is the Queen of England, she deserves that. In spite of what anyone thinks of how I bring her up I have this to say; it is our life and if I choose to shower my child with the best, who are you to judge. I am blessed to have such an intelligent child. My <u>mother</u> and I always read to her. We tell her she is the smartest in the world.

We tell her she is the most blessed baby in the world. We tell her about God and that without Him you are nothing. I constantly read Bible passages to her to instill and root the word of God in her life. I make sure she knows that God is going to be in her life. I thank God everyday that I didn't abort my baby. She has shown me how to live again. As bad as she is, she brightens my day every morning when she wakes up. She always says, "Good morning Ma, I had a nice sleep." And she ends the night with reading her Bible prayer and telling me, "Don't let the bed bugs bite." It literally melts my heart away.

Taylor has a smile and personality that lights up the room. Now you know that your child is good when you have a family of a different race that falls in love with your child. Sue, Tony, and Melissa love her so much. What makes me even happier is that Taylor doesn't see white all she sees is the love that the three of them give her. I am very blessed to have them in her life. They are blessed also because they have us. They treat Taylor as if they gave birth to her themselves. Taylor loves grandma Sue and I wouldn't have it any other way. Through the time of giving birth and me being pregnant, I was with another guy. I really got with him to ticked off my ex. In the process, I forced myself to have sex with him. It was a one-time thing. I already knew I was pregnant. I couldn't have a baby by someone I ran over and tried to kill.

So I lied and told him, it was his baby. When I saw my daughter she looked just like my ex. I wasn't ready to face those facts yet, so I stood my ground and really tried to convince myself she was the other guy's child. Well we took a blood test, and the test showed what I already knew; that he was not the father. I had to do the worst, call my ex and tell him that, yes, we have a child together. I think I would have rather been beaten with a belt with ten thousand needles in the belt then dipped in a bathtub full of hot water and alcohol.

He already knew it was his child as well as I did. He would hound the other guy and tell him it's his baby, and that we were still messing around. He and I both know that wasn't true. I know what I did was wrong. I am not proud of myself. If you knew all the drama that I went through with my child's father, you probably would have done the same thing. I didn't want to spend the rest of my life having to deal with him. I never apologized to him and never will.

I know people judged me by the way that I acted. Who are they to judge? *Judge not, that ye be not judge. For what judgment you judge you shall be judged; and with what measure you mete, it shall be measured to you again.* (Matt 7:1-2) See, I had no right to sit back and judge anyone's action. Just like they had no business judging me. I knew Jesus condemned the habit of criticizing others, while I was ignoring my own faults. I had to first submit myself to God's righteous standards before attempting to examine and influence the conduct of other people. Who was I to talk about somebody when my life was hell? I wasn't in any position to talk about anybody.

I didn't know what their situation was or what they had been through. I had to remember how I felt when people would talk about me and point fingers. So I couldn't down anybody unless it was to them and I was helping them to see the negative things in their life. I had to re-examine this situation and myself. What goes around comes around. As for me and my child's father, all I can do is pray. We don't talk, he doesn't see his child or anything. He pays child support and that's because the court makes him pay. I can honestly say for five years, I have been doing it by myself. His wife, I feel, is not a real woman. A real woman is going to encourage her husband to spend time with his child. I don't have respect for neither of them. One thing I don't do is dog them in front of my child.

I will let Taylor see how her father is. Sad to say she already knows. She doesn't ask about him and she is not missing him either. I make up for what he doesn't do. I nurture and support her. I am at every school event, Karate match or church event. I am the one who is there. Not her worthless father. What's so sad is, I see history repeating itself with these no good daddies.

My father wasn't there and neither is hers. I plan to break the curse right here. My child will have a Father. As a matter of fact, she has had the best Father anybody could ask for. She calls her Father night or day, and there is nothing too hard for her Father. God is my child's Father; always have and always will be. Like I told him, we don't need you. We have everything that we need and more. One day, when he wakes up and sees that he has missed out on the best days of her life, he will regret it. I pray everyday he regrets it. The good thing about my child, since I have rooted the Bible into her, she is going to forgive him. Me on the other hand, it is going to take much prayer to ever forgive how he has treated my child.

While all the paternity issues were going on, I let some females, who meant me no good, break up a friendship between my best friend and I. I was deceived by people who meant me no good. After I came to my senses, I had to apologize to my friend and we talked about a lot of things. I let months turn into years between us. I felt empty on the inside, and knew it was time to save our friendship. The both of us are very stubborn. When I realized my girl was gone and not here with me reality kicked in. The good thing about me growing up was, I was mature enough to admit I was wrong. It took me a lot of time to swallow my pride to call Mandy and say, "Hey I was wrong."

I had reached a point where I didn't have anybody to call and just talk to. I didn't have my friend to argue with and that tore me up inside. I was tired of trying to once again camouflage my feelings when I knew I was partly to blame. Most of all, I was hurt because my friend who I thought would always be there was leaving me. Mandy had planned to go to Korea for a year to visit her boyfriend. Deep down inside I didn't want her to go. I tried to talk her out of going. Although, I knew she was missing her boyfriend, but all I could think about was my feelings.

I found the littlest reason to hate her. When the opportunity knocked I opened the door without thinking. After Mandy and I fell out, I found ways to hate her. I saw it wasn't right, or that it wasn't working, and I called my best friend. My own selfishness caused me to miss out on the months we could have had together before she left. Not to mention, all the time I wasted being angry for nothing. Since our friendship has turned back to normal, I have learned how to cope with my best friend being away. We talk almost daily along with sending crazy e-mails to each other.

In my eyes, I couldn't ask for a better friend. Besides when I am feeling lazy who else was going to do my hair, or go shopping with me? I still miss her and wish she was here. She has her own life and family. I had to come to understand that just because she isn't here doesn't mean I don't have my friend. I guess I miss her because who else could I find to do my dirt with (two words Uncle Buck, smile). My religion has and will always be a part of my life. Even when I was out in the streets, I kept God near and dear to me.

I come from what I know to be one of the best preachers and teachers in the world. Bishop Odis and First Lady Brenda Floyd have been a great inspiration in my life. I have never met two of the most caring and loving people who are not snobby or to busy to hear a problem that you have or need to talk about. They've been there for me and my family. They are two special people that I feel very close to.

Just to know I have the support from them, and knowing that what happened wouldn't be the talked around the church just overwhelmed me. Like all churches, you have your ups and downs. You have people who are always going to gossip about you whether it's good or bad. Like always, I was the negative person that people talked about. It use to bother me in the past, because I knew I wasn't as bad as people thought I was. When you have been abused and hurt so bad, what's the sense of being nice or smiling or trying to have conversations with the people whom you know are dogging you?

I was always involved in church. Whether it was the choir, Usher Board, or youth department. As I got older I strayed from church. I had gotten to the point where I was just tired of people talking about me. Instead of going to another church, I just left. Then I found myself needing church more than ever in my life. Religion was a big part of our family. Every morning before I left my mother would make me read Psalms 91, and she would pray with me.

At the time, I didn't know why she made me do this. When I found myself in a jam I would always recite that scripture and it seemed as if God heard me and got me out of that situation. I left the church for a while. I admit I used to get mad when people would talk about my church. I always protected my church no matter what people thought or said that was my church and I was proud of it. There was one Minister that really got me back on track. He helped me turn my situation around. I remember when I was in high school I used to skip school and go to a house down the street from his. I was outside smoking a blunt. He rode down the street and looked right at me. First thing I said, I know he was going to tell my mother he saw me. That Sunday in church, out of nowhere he spoke to me. I was like hi. He just walked away. I just kept saying I know he knew that was me. Anyway, I guess you could say he saw something special in me. My mother always told me I had a calling on my life. At the time I didn't want to accept that. He would minister to me and always prophesy into my life. Everything he told me always came to pass.

I talked with him on a daily basis. As I started to talk with him we developed a relationship that turned into a friendship, which lead me to trust again. He opened my eyes and heart so that I could see the things God wanted me to fulfill in my life. He showed me how to pray and how to get my prayers answered. He taught me how my tongue was very powerful and I should watch what and how I say things to people. He encouraged me to trust God and to stand on His word and, if I did, God would never fail me. I opened my heart, mind, and soul to Him. I trusted in Him and He never let me down.

I looked up to the minister as a father. He is a man who is strong, knew the word, and walks in it. I have to be honest he made me want to live like he is. The anointing is all over him. Most of all, the way he is makes me want a husband with the same qualities he has. He treats his wife like a queen. The minister showed me the things I did wrong and the things I did right. I always thank God for placing him in my life.

The minister never stopped hounding me until I caught on to the Word and understood it. There is a verse in the Bible that reminds me of him, and some of my other friends. (Proverbs 18:24) *A man that hath friends must show himself friendly; and there is a friend that sticketh closer than a brother.* I love the Minister for being there, helping me, and most of all for lending a listening ear, and showing me what a father is suppose to be like.

Out of everything he did for me, I thank him for showing me how a man should be. When I strayed from the church the devil was right in my ear, and I could literally feel his breath on the back of my neck telling me that God isn't real. He would say just look at your life; you've been molested, rape, dogged, betrayed and lied to.

He told me I was nothing. I fed into that and I felt that maybe he was right. Why would God have me go through all those things at such a young age? Why would He take my cousin from me when she was just a little person not giving her a chance at life? Why would He have my father not be in my life? Why? I didn't know at the time, He was leading me to be a testimony for someone else.

I felt so betrayed by God, and I was very angry. I felt like He cared nothing about me. If He did, He wouldn't let all those bad things happen to me. I really wanted to call it quits and just die. I was tired of the fight and the struggle. I really tried to get the evil thoughts. I knew none of the things that the devil was telling me was true. My pastor was always telling us that God never puts more on us than we can bear. Meaning God knows how far to push you until He has your attention.

Knowing that this was a season I was going through and that I would come out on top. I wanted to be on top as the victor not the one who got defeated. So I read my Bible, I cried out to the Lord to please help me. I said to the Lord, Guide me oh thou great Jehovah feed me till I want no more. I believed in God, once again, that He would Guide me, and feed me His word, till I wanted no more. Getting pregnant was the turning point in my life. It turned me back to church, gave me a new look on life, and it made me want to change my life.

More than anything, I wanted to start with the youth in the church, especially with the young ladies. We have this ministry called BAD (Beautiful Anointed Daughters). More than anything, I wanted to be part of that. The person was over it said that I couldn't for whatever reason she had. I felt that she just didn't like me. I must admit I was very angry. I felt who was she to say I can't join a ministry in the church. It hurt me because I had so much to offer these young ladies, yet my voice would never be heard. I knew that all the things that I had been through was a testimony to someone, and they needed to know all the dangers that was out there.

As bad as I wanted to leave the church again, I stuck it out, because I knew I had tried to do my part to let my voice be heard. I feel it is more than just having dinners, taking them shopping, and on trips. That's fine, but who is woman enough to tell them about sex, STD's, betrayal, death, drugs, good guys and bad guys, and most of all, how to live a Godly life? No longer do I hold a grudge against the person who turned me away, when I wanted to be apart of the church. See, there is a part of me growing up. I still speak and talk to her. I won't let me hating her send me to hell.

I had to be woman enough to call her, tell her I was sorry, and would she forgive me? I was letting people influence me to hate more and more. Well, I shouldn't say people it was only one person. I have been reborn and from here on out, I will make sure I will be heard from the youth around me; even if I can't be heard from the youth in my church. That is a promise that I have made to myself. My mother is a woman that I will fight for everyday of my life. It seems as soon as you are over one obstacle, another one is waiting for you.

VIII
Unraveling The Pain

The music that I was addicted to was no good for me. I remember when Esham came to the Capitol Theatre in Flint. I was in the front row cheering him on. I was stuck on his words, till I was living them. I found myself talking the same language he was talking. My brain and my conscious mind were in constant conflict. My conscious mind would tell me you shouldn't be listening. I would throw the conscious mind out the window and let my brain enjoy the evil thoughts that were going through my mind. Which made it even harder. My mind had been rooted into God since I was a child. The problem that I had was, I was angry. Angry with some of my family, angry with these sorry guys I was dealing with. Most of all, I was angry with me. I didn't like myself.

I hated what I had become, and I hated how my cousin took advantage of me. I was angry that I didn't have the nice shape that all the guys wanted. I was always looked at as one of the guys. I wanted to be more than one of the guys. I wanted to appear sexy and attractive to them. Not to be called when the game was on to sit back, smoke, and drink a couple of rounds. I wanted them to see something more than just that. At the time I could stay out as late as I wanted. I would lie and say I was over so and so house, or tell my mom, I am hanging with this person. I became depressed. There were a lot of guys that I never had enough courage to approach. When I got older they approached me, and after a while, I was glad I didn't have the courage to approach them. Some of our black men are so sorry. Black women don't make it any better, because we let these guys run us over and talk down to us.

We cause our own abuse. I will be glad when we as black women decide we will not take their mess anymore. One thing I did learn in high school, with friends, boyfriends, and drugs was that I wasn't happy with none of it. So I did things that I thought would make me happy. It never occurred to me that everything I did would have a consequence, and I would have to stand up and accept my punishment when I got caught. It really didn't matter to me. What I thought was love and respect from people was really hatred, dishonesty, and most of all fear. The fear of who I knew, and what they knew, carried dire consequences.

During my 10th year of high school, one of my teachers was always getting on me about my attitude. One day she talked to me about the trouble I was getting into. I was skipping school, smoking, yelling down the halls, and just being a menace. She said, "Why do you do the things that you do?

Pretty girls don't walk the halls cursing, and keeping up mess the way that you do. How would you feel it, if you had a daughter who was doing some of the things that you are doing? Would it please you that your child was walking in the same path you?" She said, "The problem is you don't love yourself, and people see that you don't love yourself. So if you can't love you, why should they?" I told her, I didn't want to be loved. I would rather those h--s fear me than love me. I get more respect that way. She looked at me and said, "I will pray the Lord doesn't hold you responsible for the things that you say, but I know you know better." I had told her, "If the Lord cared so much why is the world like this? People misuse and abuse you, and hurt you so bad that you would do anything to make the pain go away. If God really loved us he wouldn't let all the evil things happen to good people like me who didn't deserve the things that happen to them.

Why would he do that to us?" She said, "It is called faith; until you decide to put your faith and trust in God bad things will always happen." I said, "That's not right." I looked at her with tears in my eyes and said, "I put my faith in Him when I was younger and He took everything from me. Who's to say it will change this time?" God had let me down time after time and year after year. I was upset with God. He let things happen to me and I didn't understand why. My world of destruction was causing my life to just go down hill. From fighting, in jail, and using drugs. To top it all off, I started drinking real heavy too. I was hopeless. I knew that it would have to be God, Himself, to turn me around, because I wasn't going to do it on my own. There was just so much my mother could do. I am surprise my mother still have knees the way she used to pray for me.

Putting me on punishment didn't do a thing but make me rebel more. The more I rebelled, the angrier I became. I would wait until she left for work and leave the house at one and two in the morning. I would hang out or go on a booty call, when I should have been at home getting a good night sleep for school. I remember I used to steal my uncle's car. He would be downstairs high and drunk. I would take his keys and cruise the town or go see some of my male friends. Sometimes I would go to the club. I did that for about a year or two before I finally got caught. I will never forget that day. It was the weekend of the pajama jam at CLC.

That was a skating rink everybody went to. I had told my friend that I would pick her up and we were going. We were out of school for Christmas break. I was on punishment again for something I'd done. Well I had opened up some of my gifts that had my new Fila coat, outfit, and shoes. I was dressed and ready to go. I went downstairs to get my uncle's keys and I was out the door. I never made it to CLC, I had detoured somewhere else. When I returned, I had gotten a nail in the tire, which I did not know. I pulled into the driveway and noticed that My Uncle Robert's car was in the driveway. My heart was pounding a million miles an hour. They opened the door and the only thing I could hear was, *"I am telling your mother on you."*

I spent all night thinking about what was going to happen to me. When my mother got home, I lied and told her I was talking to my friend on the phone who was in the hospital and the phone went dead. I told her I thought something had happened to her. My mother beat the hell out of me. Once again, I was on punishment. I was doing all this driving without a license. A lot of people were telling my mother that I would grow out of it. To just let me go and, eventually, I would get tired of doing the same thing, hanging with the same crowd, and getting into the same trouble. As I saw it, that is what I wanted to do. I felt they were my friends and they cared about me. They had my back, and they were down for me. Eventually, I did grow up and came back to reality. I knew it would have to take something drastic in my life for me to change. Back in school they called me Looney. People thought I was the craziest female on earth. It was nothing for me to kick somebody's butt or curse them out.

I remember an incident in 1994, where this girl really didn't like me for whatever reason. I was walking home from school and this girl that didn't like me approach me. She was a big girl and I wasn't even trying to fight her. While we were wrestling, I managed to get my knife and I poked her in the leg with it. (One good thing my father ever did for me was give me a knife). I ran home with bricks in my stomach scared to death. I just knew I was going to jail. I cried all night worried about what would happen to me in the next 24 hours. For the next couple of months I was on edge not knowing what was going to happen to me. I hid that knife over a friend's house. Every time I went out to the club, I had that knife with me. Until one night the security guard searched me, he found my knife and took it. He said he would give it back to me after the club closed.

A fight broke out, and there was so much confusion that I left without my knife. Which was probably a good thing, because that knife would have gotten me into a lot of trouble. Now clubbing that was my spot. I was in the club Monday through Sunday. I would leave church on Sunday night go home get dressed, roll my weed and head to the club with my girls. In this one club you could smoke your weed, toot your cane or whatever. This club was also known for people always getting their head cracked, having shoot outs, or whatever you felt like doing. It was the worst club in Flint (The Beaver's).

I remember back in 1999 my girl was having her party at this club. Now there was a gang of us. Dressed to strictly impress; Leather and Coogi, we were looking good. Around 12:30 or 1:00 a.m. a big fight broke out. I mean tables and chairs were flying and blood was everywhere. Instead of us trying to leave, we just stood on top of one of the tables watching the fight.

In the summer of 1999, some friends and I were hanging outside the MC Breed Concert. This one girl (my stepfather use to date her mother) came outside. She and I always had problems. From trying to run each other off the road, to slashing tires, and busting out windows. It was always a war with us. I was high and drunk as usual, and was not about to put up with her mess. Now, the girls I normally hung out with were inside the Concert, and I came down with my cousin and her friends. Before I knew it punches were being thrown, the girl I didn't like was being choked on a pole, mace was getting sprayed and people were going to jail. That was a night I will never forget.

In the beginning, I never knew what kind of impact my behavior had on other people. No one knew about the hurt, deceit, and heartache I was enduring. So many times I wanted to die. No one really knew that the way I was acting, really was not me. It was as if I was possessed with a spirit that I just couldn't shake off me.

The question is, did I want to shake it? I knew deep down in my heart I was not the fighting type. I would never fight back when I was little. If the girls really knew what I was thinking before I was getting ready to fight they probably would have left me at home. Being pushed so much to my limits, I became a fighter. When I was younger, I got tired of my mother fussing about me not hitting people back when they hit me. So eventually, I got to the point to where I was always fighting. Deep down inside, I really wanted to talk out the problem and find out everybody was so angry. Unfortunately, I had the same problem they had, so who was I to judge and try to make amends.

I hated fighting, I hated arguing, and most of all, I hated hanging with the bad influences that I was hanging with. What was I suppose to do? Tell them I can't hang with you because you fight too much. I wondered what is my reason, and soul purpose for being here? God must have had a purpose because I am still here. Really it was not by choice. Until this day, no one knew I attempted to kill myself at school. A girl that stayed in a dorm room (down the hall) found me and took me to the hospital. I took a lot of Tylenol. I just wanted to sleep away. Not to mention, the other students thought I was totally insane.

Which I wasn't, I was just at the end of my ropes. I spent two days in the hospital wondering what is left in my life for me to do? Not to mention, the thoughts that were roaming through my mind constantly. I often thought about my cousin Nailah, who had died. Most of all, I thought about the child that I aborted. You see my past is based on more than just my destruction. It is based on someone who I thought I could trust. Once again, I was put into a position in which I couldn't trust anymore. Again, I was raped and violated. I was tormented, hurt, and confused. I was pregnant and never told a soul.

Again, I was scared, hurt and didn't know what to do. I was in the process of telling Felisha, but she made a comment about me being an international player when my pager went off. For some reason, it sent me through the roof. I started to cry. No one understood what was wrong with me, and I couldn't tell anyone. At that moment, I started to hate and resent her. I had so much hurt and anger till I could have choked the life out of her. I really felt if she knew me she should have realized something was wrong. I couldn't blame that on her. My mother never realized my cousin was raping me. So how could I be upset with her.

Months passed and I was beginning to show. I dropped a bowling ball on my stomach numerous of times. I had done everything that I could to lose this baby, but nothing worked. When I felt it moving it made me sick to my stomach. I would get mad every time the baby moved. I would punch myself in the stomach to make it stop. My mother, was snooping in my room, found out when she saw a letter I addressed to my cousin.

In the letter: *I was telling my perverted cousin, how once again he had violated me but this time I had gotten pregnant by the pervert. I told him that when he got out of jail, I was going to kill him. I took the Bible verses and used it for my advantage.* In (Exodus 21:24-25) it says, *"eye for a eye, tooth for tooth, hand for hand, foot for foot, burning for burning, wound for wound, and stripe for stripe." I added my own verse, molestation equals a murder. I hated what he did to me and how I was not in control. In my eyes, he had all the power and control over me, and I was about to put an end to it. I had a gun that I got from a guy. It was a throw-a-way.*

The guy said, use it once and get rid of it. I was going to take the gun and throw it into Devil's Lake where it belonged. I was going to kill him at our family dinner. I wanted him to tell everyone what he had done to me. I wanted him to beg for my forgiveness and plead for his life. I wanted him to see what it felt like not to have control over your situation. I wanted him to feel shameful for what he had done. When I felt he was sorry, I was going to pull the trigger and shoot him right between the eyes. *He was going to die because I felt I had the right, according to what the Bible said.*

I was so confused and lost. I didn't know where to turn. I never got the chance to kill him. He left to go to the store and never returned. He had gotten caught doing something and he was in jail. God spared his life from me. That really pissed me off. I felt jail was too good for him. Even death was too good, but at least he couldn't hurt another child. I always hoped he got raped in jail, then he would know what it felt like to have something taken from you. I wanted him to think how it would feel, if had a daughter and she had been used the way he used me.

Could he bare the pain that a parent would feel knowing their child had been violated? What would his response be? Could he forgive and let it go? Or would he want revenge like I did? After my mother saw the letter she took me to have an abortion at six months of being pregnant. It took me a while to understand how she could forgive him? When my mother told his mother what had happened, she believed me right off the back. The same thing that happened to me happened to her by her stepfather. She knew what I was feeling and what I was going through. Depression on top of depression filled my body even more.

If you have ever had an abortion, then you know how I felt. I was hurting. I had killed a human being who didn't have any idea why they were killed. I couldn't love something that made me feel robbed of being a woman. I couldn't look at that tiny face and give it the care that it needed. I felt so empty and trashy. I thought people were pointing their fingers at me. I was ready to kill everybody that had deceived me, and didn't care about the consequences.

Well, that's when all the news hit the fan. In the letter I had written, my mom found out that my cousin had been raping me all these years. At that time, I wasn't ready to talk about it. I wasn't ready to forgive, and I wasn't done being angry. My mother sent me to a shrink. I hated that lady. She was the nosiest person I had ever met in my life. I felt that, if you haven't gone through what your patient has how can you help them? You haven't been violated, so there is nothing you can possibility tell me to help me through this. The things she wanted to talk about did not pertain to what I was going through. So I stopped going. I hated my life and the things that were going on in it. My mother and I were not as close as I would have liked.

Basically, I blamed her for the things that had happened to me. I felt she should have known about the things my cousin was doing to me. Most of all, I hated the way she sheltered me. I had to always lie about where I was going because I was usually going somewhere that she didn't like. It was hard; I never really had the courage to tell my mother that, now that I am an adult, some decisions in my life was for me to decide and not her. I really wanted to be part of my father's life, but couldn't because I didn't want my mom to think I didn't need her anymore. Also since, he was never in my life, I could not understand why she didn't want me around him.

I love my mother. She has really been my provider since I have been in this world. She bent over backwards to make sure I have everything I need. She tried to keep me away from danger, but I wanted to be around it. Most of all, she instilled Christ into my life and prayed with me every morning before school. When my cousin was doing all the hateful things he did to me, I blamed her.

I felt she should have known. She never saw the changes that I was going through, and I felt she should have. Once she noticed the changes and saw the horrible things I was doing, she sent me to a shrink. Once again, I resented her. It wasn't nothing that a shrink could help me with. I needed to talk and get my anger and frustration out. I wanted to shout and yell and get a lot of things off my chest, I needed to cry, I needed to be held, not to talk to a stranger that I knew nothing about.

I wanted my mother to understand, it wasn't a doctor that I needed it was always her. I felt she should have made me talk and tell her what was going on in my life. She should have asked me why couldn't I have good relationships with people? Why was it so hard for me to keep a boyfriend? I wanted her to feel the pain that I was living through day in and day out. I still love my mom. As I got older, I couldn't blame her for what she never had a clue about. When I was getting raped, that was something that was really hidden in the closet. In the '80s, you never would have thought about someone raping your child. It was a topic that was never disclosed.

My mother never imagined my cousin was violating me. So how could I imagine being upset with my mother over something she never knew was happening to me. When I was in school and away from home, I felt it was my escape. I wasn't dealing with the people that had hurt me. It was my way of having a piece of me leaving all the madness. I was forced to go and talk to a professional about what was going on in my life. My counselor thought it would be a good idea. She was so wrong.

I was sent to a male counselor who was just as nosey as the other one. I felt what I was going through was none of his business either, so I just stopped going. Once again, I was forced to hold all my frustrations in and fight to live another day. After all the things that were going on, I just felt I needed to get away from everything. I never liked school because I still had difficulty understanding things right off. Other students always snickered and make fun of me, when I would ask questions that they felt was stupid. So instead of me asking questions, I would just sit there in silence or even slept through class just so I wouldn't hear the kids making fun of me.

One day while I was away at school I found out I had a learning disability. I was ashamed, I felt really dumb and didn't want anyone to know. I was embarrassed, and instead of getting help, I left school. I didn't want anyone to know that I learned differently than everyone else. I was not the type of person who could study and comprehend day-to-day things. I could look at things or even hear someone explain something one time, then I would understand and master it. Things were natural once I saw it. That was the way I learned.

All my life in school I was a failure, I never did anything right. All I got was Cs, Ds and Es and I wasn't happy with that. I wanted to do better, I wanted my mother to be able to brag to her friends about how good her child was doing but she couldn't because my grades were never good. Don't think I didn't try to help myself because I did. I would ask questions and try to get help but it was like the teachers didn't care whether or not I understood the lesson. Their only concern was getting a paycheck.

Before I could really get the courage and the help I needed, it was too late because I had already flunked the 12th grade. I couldn't tell my mother, I had flunked. So I ran away from home. Before I left, I wrote my mother this letter it read:

"Dear Ma, I feel that you have raised me all the years that you had to. You have done a wonderful job. I want you happy. It is time you had a life of your own like you've always wanted. Don't worry about me. I am in good hands. I'm with a lady that is 47. I want you to enjoy life. I am still going to college in August. Don't worry, you don't have to pay for it. I need to find out what the real world has to offer. Faye, I love you so much. It is time that I grew up and start taking care of myself.

I am still in Flint. You know how to get in touch with me. P.S. I am going to show you, I can do anything as long as I put my mind to it."

My fathers ex wife called my mother the next morning to let her know where I was. I always wondered what was going through my mother's mind to know that I had left home and flunked the 12th grade. It hurt me not to walk with my class and get to experience what it would feel like shaking hands with the principal and receiving my diploma in the other hand. When my mother caught up with me the next day I was sleep. She came into the room I was in and said let's go home. I was terrified. She went up to the school and talked to the principal.

He made the suggestion that I walk with my class and go to summer school when it starts. My mother felt it was too embarrassing and said no she'll just go to summer school. Little did she know, I was already facing embarrassment. I had to go to summer school, once again, I was embarrassed. Each day I just wanted to take a gun and blow my head off so I wouldn't listen to the laughs and jokes people made about me. I hated the stares and the questions people asked as to why I was in summer school.

Well, after all the humiliation that I had gone through, I graduated in August. When it was finally over, I was happy. Still, I wasn't happy with me. What could I do to better myself and most of all make my mother finally proud of me? After all the colleges that I'd gone through whether; they were community colleges, private colleges, or universities, I decided that college was not for me. It was too fast pace for me. Once I discovered I had a learning disability, I took it upon myself to get me some serious help. I had people tutor me, and I got a lot of help on the Internet. There were people who actually took the time to explain things and show me what I was doing right or wrong.

When I thought I was finally ready, I enrolled in a Business School. And would you believe it, I actually excelled. I graduated with a 91.19% overall average. I earned my degree in Medical Office Administration. I was so happy. Finally I had done something that made me proud, and most of all, I had done something so my mother could have bragging rights. I graduated with honors. My Uncle Robert from Texas surprised me and flew in for my graduation. I was very excited.

It felt so good to walk across the stage to get something that I had worked so hard for and that I had earned. That was the happiest day of my life. With all the episodes going on, I still knew that I had problems. I wasn't ready to face those facts yet. At times, I would just sit and wonder what else could go wrong in my life? I was really hoping nothing. Could this finally be my time to sit back and really look over the years, and see where I went wrong? It was time out for the self-pity because I had a mind of my own.

Basically it was time for me to face facts that I had messed up my life, and now it was time for me to take control of it. I finally realized that the people I was blaming really had nothing to do with what I was going through.

I had to reach deep down inside and find me, Naikiea Monique Jones. Really, I didn't know this person. It was going to be an adventure finding her. Once I started to see who she really was, I liked her. She is a warm, sweet, kind hearted person who would give and has given, her last to anybody. No longer was she going to continue to let people use her. No longer was she going to blame everyone else for her mistakes. No longer was she going to have self-pity parties with drugs and alcohol. She was going to be an open-minded, forgiving, loving, and caring mature adult. That is the person that I love till this day. I never understood why people could hurt other people.

I always found it to be amazing on how you can give and give until you can't give anymore. Then once you feel that you can't get hurt or burned anymore someone is always there knocking on the door. I wondered what was it about me that would make people to want to use me as a door mat that they kept wiping their feet on? I made a list of the relationships I had with females. I weighed the things I did, the way I was always there, and the way I stood by their side no matter what. Versus, how I was treated in the end. As I listed my so called friends, the list got shorter and shorter. When I was done, I only had five real friends.

I thought you should be happy. Happiness wasn't what I felt, it was depression. I couldn't understand how you could give your all to a person and they turn around and spit in your face. I compare my hurt to someone spitting in your face, because I always looked at spitting as the worst thing you could do to a person. Well, that is until I figured out, I was being betrayed for so many years. Till this day, I still couldn't tell what hurts the most. Being raped by my cousin or not being wanted by my father. Or being hurt by someone you gave your all to. Once again, I was faced with asking God why are You dumping on me?

Haven't I been through enough? I know the Lord won't put more on you than you can bear. I was at the end of my rope hanging on by a thread. Why is it always me? Why is God always trying to break me? I was holding on to the little sanity that I had left, and I felt He knew that. I always thought if I could get through the other stuff, I could get through this. I was tired of crying, tired of drinking and tired of all the problems. I needed a small break and needed it fast. I never understood why people had to encounter pain in their life.

I always felt God created the world good. Why would He let the pain come into the world? I am not God and will never be able to understand His logic. One day I would love to. I've always tried to hide my feelings and emotions around people that I saw and talked with on a daily basis. I thought they saw right through me, once they uncovered the hurt they discovered I wasn't as strong as I pretended to be. It was as if I was being fake about myself and trying to hide when I was going through rough times. When my friends were having hard times, it seemed as if I was having more hard times than they.

So I would put my feelings aside and try to be there for my friends, because that's what a true friend does. I always thought I could handle myself in any situation. I saw that it was kicking my tail. I never understood why people could hurt other people. How you could put all your trust in someone and just like that, you don't trust them anymore. That is painful. And for anyone who has ever trusted and gotten hurt here is a piece of advice. *"You might find an apple that has a worm in it, but you throw it away and just trust that the next one doesn't."*

What I'm trying to say is, *"don't risk something good on one rotten apple that you had. With all the rotten apples out there you are bound to find a good one."*

IX
Recognizing Pitfalls

The molestation caused many emotional problems throughout my life. There are times I find myself crying day and night. I have difficulty maintaining relationships with men. I don't trust men. It is hard for me to commit. I find reasons to break off relationships. I find fault with the other person instead of myself. Trying to put the molestation behind me was very difficult. It made me feel like all guys are the same. No matter how well a guy treated me the pass would always get in the way. Always in the back of my mind there remained the question, Why? What is the catch? Why would a man choose to be with a woman who could not give him her all? Why would a man want to be close to me? I wondered if they could see the hurt and pain, I was going through.

Every adult sexual experience I had with a man always brought me back to the days of being molested. Every time I would try to block out the past, I would go through an emotional break down. I became so frustrated with continuously having the same setback with men. It was difficult even when it came to someone I really wanted to be with. I wanted to feel like I was normal. I wanted to feel compassion and show them love. If was very hard for me to say, I love you. It seemed like when I did, I always got my feelings hurt. I wanted to be able to express myself and trust people. Most of all, I didn't want to worry about them hurting me. I always prayed for God to help me and take the pain away.

In (Jeremiah 8:11) it says, *For they have healed the hurt of the daughter of my people slightly, saying, Peace, peace; when there is no peace.*

Even though I was going through the hurt in my life I still had peace. God always made a way for me. Many times I was too stubborn to realize it.

Through the guidance of the Holy Spirit I stopped wondering about the problem. It was time for me make some choices. My first solution was for me to let go of the pass. I had to deal with what happened to me. Although I had been on a road to hell, in spite of it all I overcame the madness.

In (I John 4:4) it says, *Ye are of God, little children and have overcome them; because greater is He that is in you, than he that is in the world.*

The Holy Spirit knew I would overcome the evil in this world. Through Christ we can overcome sin, Satan, trial, temptation and sorrow. Through God's word I discovered I could victoriously achieve His will for my life.

In (I John 5:2) it says, *he that hath life; and he that hath not the Son of God hath not life.*

Once I understood what this scripture meant I realized God was with me all the time. I always had God in my heart. Jesus is the way the truth and the lift.

Through reading the Word of God, I began to accept the things that I could not change. I started to like the person I'd become. I no longer worry about who liked me or who didn't. I put it into my heart that I was going to have the mentality of Job. When the devil destroyed Job's family and brought sickness on him, he still trusted in God.

In (Job 13:15) it says, *though he slay me, yet will I trust Him; I will maintain mine own ways before Him.*

Even though God allowed everything that happened in my life; I still believe He will not fail me. Through His amazing grace I am still here today. I trust the Lord completely. No matter what people may say or feel about me. I am still going to be me. With the help and strength of God, I have overcome many pitfalls. I will continue to life my life to the fullest. I am an overcomer. I have recognized my pitfalls and I am letting go of the pass by striving towards the mark of a higher calling in Christ Jesus.

X
Overcoming Adversities

In 2003, I had been resurrected from the old me and now the real Naikiea is here. Now to like me is to know me. For people who don't know me: I am a person of strong opinions and I express my views energetically and often dramatically. I am an entertaining speaker and will embellish or exaggerate in order to get my point across. I have an aptitude for storytelling and performing. I have an abundance of creative ideas. I have powerful emotional attachments to the past, my family, my childhood, and places I associate with safety and security. Maintaining a connection with my roots and heritage and keeping family bonds strong are very important to me. I am loyal, devoted and sentimental. I tend to cling to whatever is dear to me. Be it people, familiar faces, or cherished possession.

I am sympathetic, nurturing, supportive, and sensitive to the emotional needs of other people. I like to be needed, to care for other, and I often worry about the people I love. I have a very strong need for a sense of belonging and acceptance, and I center much of my life around home. I am more concerned about people and their feelings with power, achievement, or position in society. Kindness, consideration, and tenderness impress me more than any honor the world can give me.

Primarily my views are often dominated by my feelings and by my own personal experiences, rather than reason, logic or abstract principles. I take things very personally, and sometimes build a wall to protect myself from pain and rejection. I feel rather shy and vulnerable at heart. I also tend to be moody experiencing frequent emotional ups and downs. I need to have a place and time to withdraw, introspect, dream, and replenish myself: otherwise I become cranky and unhappy with those around me. I function in an instinctive, non-rational manner. I like to immerse myself in creative activities where I can express my feelings, imagination, and instincts.

My compassion, sensitivity, and imagination are my strong points. My faults include an ability to release the past and go forward, clannishness, prejudice, and a tendency to be self-pitying when I meet hardships in life. I tend to be a bit stubborn and like things done my way. I love Tupac, Mary J. Blige, Jada Pinkett Smith, and Sharon Stone. The music they talk about or roles they play remind me of my life. I sleep with my TV on, because I am afraid of the dark. I watch reruns of The Cosby show, Fresh Prince, and Roseanne. I like to talk to my friends on the phone about nothing. I love to cook. I am terrified of insects. I can't swim, I am afraid of heights but like roller coasters.

I slept with my grandmother until I was 16. When I am alone I try to dance like Beyonce. I think Terrance Howard is the sexiest man alive. Why am I telling you this. I am human. I daydream just as you. I have likes and dislikes just as you. I think about being rich the same way as you. Don't think because I have been through hell and hot water, I don't wish sometimes I was someone famous. I do. I hate when people treat me like a charity case. They think because I was raped and molested my life was turned into shambles. Through it all I still have dreams. I hate for people to treat me like a handicapped person. I feel I deserve better than the fakeness that people sometimes demonstrate.

Now that you know me, I am not so bad. I no longer care what people think, or say about me because I have been raised from the dead. No longer a deadbeat that just wants to sit around and mope. I am a woman who knows what she wants and needs. I now hold my head up when I walk the streets. I am no longer ashamed of my past. Just like me everybody has a past. Now I am woman enough to let the world know what my faults and mishaps are. God had a plan for me and it wasn't for me to be six feet under. I am here for a purpose. A promise that I have made to myself is to accomplish that purpose before leaving this earth.

Everybody makes mistakes but the key is for you to learn from them. Never mind the negative talk because you are going to have that whether you are doing something positive or not. I have learned that everyone has to be themselves. Never mind the talk, stares, and comments people make about you, because if there is one thing I have learned is misery loves company. If you are with a person who is miserable, trust me, you will be miserable too. Even if I am going through trials I've learned how to say I'm blessed and highly favored in the Lord. Things really aren't as bad as they seem. My main focus in life now is God and my child.

Nothing else matters. I am living my days one day at a time with "No More Drama." I have learned how to cope with everyday life by having a meditation time where I pray and talk to the Lord about what I am going through. Notice the key word **through** because I know that the Lord is going to help me come out of this. It feels good to finally be able to have a good clear head. My head is clearer now than it has been in years. I faced my fear and got a lot of things off my chest. I finally went to my cousin's house and confronted him about what I was feeling and going through. I made him listen and I made him see how it feels to be betrayed.

September 20, 2002, it was my first official day of being an educated mature woman. I didn't know what to expect when I got there. I really went to tell his wife what he did so she would know what she was married to? I wanted her to know her husband was a child molester and she needs to beware for her children. When I got there it went a whole different direction. I don't have to hold on to old memories. I was big enough to let bygones be bygones. I forgave him and yes, I will try this trust thing again.

Some people might think I'm crazy for letting things that happen to me be forgotten. They aren't forgotten the pain is still there as well as the memory. That is a pain and memory I no longer need in my life. Most of all, I don't give two dead flies what people say or think. I'm moving forward not backwards. This is now my public apology to everyone. Anything that I have done to anyone and it has hurt you, I am truly sorry. For anyone who really knows me, if I can forgive than you can forgive. Unforgiveness and holding on to things was one attribute, I had to let go.

Now that my mind is clear, I keep my head up; always smiling, and most of all keep all the negative energy out of my life. No longer am I looking for that dropdead fine man that I want because he is cute. I want that man who will do right by me. I want a supportive, trustworthy, dependable, loving, wise educated man who will love me in spite of my past. One thing that is true is beauty is only skin deep. It's what's in a person heart that matters. I would be happy with a man who treats me like a queen. Than a man who is fine, who treats me like the neighborhood crack friend. And to everyone who said I would not amount to anything, I have four words for you **Look at me now.** One thing standing in the way of my success is my father not being a part of my life. Personally, it will probably be God to bring us together. Until then, I am still happy.

Who knows maybe one day we will have the relationship, I have always wanted. Until that day comes, I will always love my father; although I don't like some of the things that he does. Hopefully, something will happen in his life that will give him peace. I desire that everybody is happy and successful in everything they do. That they have everything that their hearts and minds could ever dream of. You can have it all, if you just keep your faith in God and not let the negativity that surrounds you, take your mind or your main priority. As for my one special friend that has been in my life since day one protecting me. You are truly a best friend any woman could ever have, and one of the reasons besides God I am here today. Kyle, I will always love and respect you. I wish nothing but the best for you and your family.

Having my daughter was a major turning point in my life. Watching her grow up is causing me to be more protective. I never want the same thing happen to my child. Therefore, I am teaching her to speak out. I missed out on a gift. It was hard learning how to love myself. Now I love myself more than any amount of money, anyone could ever give me. I don't regret my past. It has made me who I am today.

In June 2005, my mother wrote a letter of apology to me. When I read the letter it was like she had been reading my mind. It touched my heart deeply. It let me really know that there is a God and that He had been listening to me.

This is what the letter said:

In this lifetime as you grow wise and older you have to take responsibility for you life whether good or bad. I have not been as good a Mother according to the Bible. There comes a time, you have to face your mistakes and ask for forgiveness no matter how old you are or who the person is. So, I come to you in the name of our Lord and Savior Jesus Christ and ask you for forgiveness.

> *For being a stupid mother*
> *Not teaching you about life and what you would face*
> *For not protecting you and putting you in harms way and in the enemy's way.*

I never really said anything to you but I had no idea your cousin was raping you, and doing ungodly things to you and making your life miserable. You should have been protected from that and I take full responsibility for that. For not seeing and being a stupid mother. It was not your fault but mine. Monique you are very special for that task and I want you to know you did pass the test.

God is going to honor you for that mark my words. Myself and other girls could not have handled that. You see it now how young girls are so messed up because someone violated their bodies or mistreated them. Some girls never recover they are all messed up until adulthood. God did grace you so don't be ashamed to tell that you made it. It will help somebody else. You can help save them this is why young girls like you. You have a gift from God that can draw other young ladies to God and be saved. Go on and do His will for your life and it will help someone else's life. That is why Satan wants you to feel you are not worthy. You are worthy because of Jesus and you passed God's test at an early age. When everything was taken away from your youth and childhood for this I ask for forgiveness. You know Bob told me after reading the letter of what your cousin did to you that she believed you right away. Bob said, when it happened to her, no one believed her, not even her mother just granny.

I pray that your cousin repents of his sins or else he will end up in hell. (John 15:16 and Jer 1:5-9) You are a prophet sent from God, be glad He chose you. You were hand picked. Some people want God to choose them. Some go out on their own without His calling, but you were different He chose you. Accept it walk in it, because God gave it to you. Jesus died for you to have it. On more thing, I don't want the same thing to happen to Taylor. That is why I worry about where she is or who she is with. I know now by watching TV, people who have had this happen to them by a family member, or friend. I won't take that for granted like I did with you. I would have never thought it could happen, but it did. I hate it happened, we have to believe God and not let this happen to Taylor.

I don't care who the person is. Don't be stupid like me and let her go off with people or family. We don't know what is in a person's mind. So be a better protector than I was, so Taylor won't have that problem in her childhood taken from her or forced from her. You know Oprah's life was like yours raped by an uncle and God turned it into helping other women. So can you with the help of God. That is why you have been called. I want the best for you Monique. I might not have ever told you but I do. I might not ever have the husband that I want but I am willing to live a spirit filled life without a man. I don't have to have a man in my life to live a good Christian life.

So I don't worry about a man. Now I want to live a good Christian life in front of you and Taylor. I want God's blessings not man's, so I will do what ever I have to do not to plant anymore bad seeds. You and Taylor are worth it. Love Faye.

Her letter was heartfelt and just what I needed. As for my mother, she raised me to believe in God, and depend on no one but Him. Although my mom and I have had our differences, there is nothing I would change about the way she raised me. She taught me to be tough, and to stand on my own two feet and keep God first. She may think I didn't take her advice. It just took me longer to apply it. It feels so good to be renewed and to know that no matter what I did in life, she still loves me and supported me in every decision. That is worth more than winning the mega millions.

There are a few words to describe my mom. She is like a bad rainstorm with the scent of perfect red roses that would brighten any day. I love her so much. I hope *Silent Cries* will inspire, uplift and change someone's life. Remember without forgiveness there is no love.

To My Ladies

My sisters, it is time for us to stand up and take control of our lives. We no longer have to put up with these sorry men that mean us no good. Maya Angelou once told us, that we're phenomenal women and I believe that. *Destiny's Child* told us that we are survivors. We have been surviving for years without a man. Like the old saying, we can do bad all by ourselves. We don't need a man to bring us down. We are queens and it is about time that we started to act like it. Let's stop using our bodies as trashcans for these sorry men. Let's stop dogging each other and backbiting each other.

We need to finally stand up for ourselves and be real with ourselves. We need to come together as women and protect each other. How many more of our sisters have to die from the violent crime of punks who couldn't keep there hands to themselves. When are we going to say enough is enough? When can we finally say you are my sister and I have your back. How long will it be before we can say we are finally free from the drama. It is time to show our children that we are more than a late night booty call to some thug. It is time for our children to know that we're there for them. It's time for us to stop letting our children see us smoking, or cussing, or wearing clothes that are not appropriate. Let our children see us as women not hoes. A role model not a wanna be. Let our children know that we care for them and that it will stop now. Let our children know that they can be anything they want to be. All they have to do is trust God. It is time for us as women to get our priorities straight. Let us start now and save our children from anything bad that could happen if we don't step up. We as women must start to encourage, help, uplift, love and most of all be there for one another. We as a race are all we have. Let's not hurt anymore as a race, but let us heal together as a race. Let's make this nation the best nation our children could ever grow up in. Let us now stand, be women and take our lives back.

To My Brothers

My brothers, when are you going to start standing up for your women, instead of beating them down? Who is going to be the man that says enough is enough? How long do the women have to wait for you, as men to stop the hustling and the gang banging? How many more of our Black men do we have to lose to stupid violence? Which one of you is going to be man enough to put the gun down? How much longer will you sit there and keep raping and robbing your women? When will you finally say, I need to be real with the women and myself? How long will your beautiful Black sisters have to keep struggling with your children while you run the streets? When will it be the time that a woman can depend on a man to help them with their children? Why is it so hard for my brothers to be faithful? How much longer do we as women have to put up with your mess? When God created the earth He made you (man) first. What even makes a woman unique is that we were formed from your rib.

My brothers we are a part of you. It is time to love you woman, and be real to her. It is time for you as a man, to help your black women to stop struggling. It is time to let that corner go selling that crack and get a real job. Help support your women and children. It is time for you to pull your pants up and put on a nice fitted suit to make yourself look presentable. It is time to lose the braids, and lose the language of calling Black women b-----s and h---s. It is time to love your women, and stop hating on each other as a race. It is time to step up like a man and take our city, state, and nation back. It's time to show the children that daddy does care. It's time to show the women that you are there for them. It's time to show other men that violence is not the answer. It's time to stop taking the bodies of your black women and using them till you can't use them anymore. It's time for boys to step up and be men. It is now time to heal each other. It's time to make the world safer for you, your women and children. It's time to put the club down and get hype for Jesus. It is time to put the blunt down and read books to the children. It is time to put the drink down and go to church and drink the blood of the Lord. We are living in a time, where violence is taking over our communities. We are tired of losing our men to drugs, death, and jails. Let us see who will be the man that will encourage other men to be lawyers, doctors, and engineers. Let us see who will be that man. Let's wake up Black men. We as Black women need you, and even more our children do. Let's stop the hating and start to love Peace!

Author's Bio

Author Naikiea Monique Jones is an only child and a native of Flint, MI. She is a 28-year-old single parent of 5-year-old Taylor. Ms. Jones is a (CMAA) Certified Medical Administrative Assistant. She is currently enrolled in New Horizons Technology Center; studying to become a (CPC) Certified Professional Coder. She is a member of New Jerusalem Full Gospel Baptist Church, where Bishop Odis A. Floyd is her pastor. Naikiea is a very outspoken young woman who has overcome every obstacle that has come her way.

Ms. Jones is very bright, fun loving and a joy to be around. She enjoys golf and playing pool. She has performed in a play entitled, *'I'll meet you over the Rainbow.'*

Ms. Jones enjoys spending time with her daughter. She also enjoys styling and braiding hair. She recently founded *'Silent Cries Child Advocate,'* (SCCA). She is publicly speaking out about how to recognize and prevent child abuse. Ms. Jones felt compelled to get *Silent Cries* published because of the very alarming statistics: *"One out of three girls and one out of five boys are sexually abused in this country, everyday!!!!"*

How to contact the Author

Call Silent Cries Child Advocate at: (810) 908-4649
Email: Naikiea@comcast.net
Or visit her website at: www.mysilentcries.com

My Family Pictorial

Include photographs of my family, church family and friends who gave contributions, which helped me in publishing Silent Cries. I would also like to say thanks for supporting me, loving me and being there for me through all my trials. I love you all.

The Allen's: Jordan, Henderson, Tesa and Jayden

Kyle, Justin, Me, Jarell and my daughter Taylor

Author Naikiea M. Jones

Uncle Robert and Niece Naikiea

Mia, Janage and Baby Taylor

Mom, Grandma, Taylor and Me

The Floyd Family

Bishop Odis and First Lady Brenda Floyd

Me, Felisha, Heather and Taylor

Spillers   Sa`Naiyah

Me and Mandy

The Johnson's

Gwen and Robert

RJ   **Torri**

The Hollins

Shalonda

Shavonta

Shelanna

Appreciation

First, I would like to thank my Creator, my Father, and my Friend. The Almighty God, who have carried me since the womb. Who have kept me from dangers seen and unseen. I thank my mom and grandma for always loving me, in spite of the things I did. Thanks for being my solid rock and good advisors. You can never be replaced, love you always. The world's best grand father Hilton Jones.

Thanks to my three sisters who got me into more trouble than I could ever imagine; Shalonda, Shelanna, and Shavonta. Love you always.

My Uncles Robert and David; you have always been there and I thank you. Auntie Gwen, you are such an inspiration in my life, keep up the good work. The world needs more Christian women like you. Heather thanks for all the things you do for Taylor. Eric, Nerita and Jeremiah love yall. We've got some monsters on our hands.

My cousins; Mario, Denia, Darius, Barbara, Cookie, Kamona, Devon and Mike; Trecia, Carissa, and Al thanks for being part of my family.

My best friends; Kyle and Mandy; with friends like you, I don't know where I would be today. I thank you for all your love and support. Friends Forever, no matter what.

My five real friends are my sisters, and my back bone; Mia, Nikki, Jamise, Angel, Felisha. There are no words to say just how much you all mean to me. Thanks for putting up with me all these years.

My nieces; Torri, and Shanya (your mother will kill me if I didn't spell your name right).

My nephews; Jarell, Lil Anthony, RJ, Kyle, and Justin. Five of the finest men. I love yall so much.

My big brother, who I love and will beat you down to the ground if you mess with Tony Floyd. I'll always have your back no matter what. Thanks to Bishop Odis and Brenda Floyd, for being the best pastor and first lady and my second parents. Much love to you Ms. Kimmie Bowman.

My family in Cali, I know you all had no idea, I was writing a book. Sorry and I still love ya.

The Walkers and Barbers in Baton Rouge, LA; Our Chicago family, Donna, Victor, Darrin and little Victor. The Hollins in Jonesville, LA; the Payne's in Natchez, MS; The Moore, Looney, Murphy, Bowman, Spillers family in Flint, MI the Cross family in Chicago, I love you.

We have been through thick and thin but managed to hold on. My second church family Stand on the Word Ministry. My Jonesville, Louisiana family, Michelle, Mildred, Gene, Michael, and all the family. My girl Lydia. I won't tell anybody we use to be in Jonesville. Jada and little Jay. Love yall. The man who has been a father, friend, and inspiration to me Mr. Veotis L Jones. Love you, love you, love you. My special love thanks to the people who donated the money so that this book may exist. My mother Faye, granny Vernis, My uncles Robert and Gwendolyn Hollins, David Hollins. My aunt Pat Spillers. My good friend Katesa Allen. The Jung Do Martial Arts staff, Diane Stephens, Connie Brown, and Candence Burnett. Nikki, Jamise, and Tony Floyd. Minister Veotis Jones. Thank you. Without your and support and God on my side I don't how this would have happened. Thank you so much. P.S. My sister Mary J Blige you don't know you are my sister, but you are. I love you. Keep doing what you do. I will always support you. Your number one fan 1 luv.

Special thanks to my publisher for taking the time and effort to make sure *Silent Cries* is a success.

Thanks to my editor for all your hard work and suggestions. Also for making sure that I didn't let the hood come out as much.

Thanks to my little birdie Candace Burnett, it is a reason God placed you in my life. Thank you for helping me with *Silent Cries.*

Last but not least, to the man who has been a father, friend, and inspiration to me; Minister Veotis L Jones. Love you, love you, love you.

LaVergne, TN USA
28 February 2010
174455LV00003B/36/A